CW00665598

Praise for *Zizanies* (French edition):

'This essay addresses the matters of affect and unease, inviting reflection on the voice as a tool for the emancipation of the body. Through Clara Schulmann's sensibility, the words of women who speak up start disrupting the tedium of routine and wreak havoc.' – *Critique d'art*

'[*Zizanies*] reads like a thriller [...] an idiosyncratic collage, born of the critical examination of the things the author both reads and hears. In just over 200 pages, Schulmann spans a vast imaginary community; bringing together innumerable feminist figures – from the well-known to the unrecorded, to the unexpected. [...] Situating the act of expression is at the centre of Schulmann's project, convinced as she is of the need to include the colours of emotion, one's words' occasional fragility and awkwardness, and the gentle curiosity that motivate her research in the articulation of her thoughts and ideas. The aim is to free herself from the constraints of academic writing and to find a freer hybrid form, while preserving the richness and precision of her references.' – *The Art Newspaper*

'A veritable mille-feuille of moods, allusions and digressions.' – *Switch*

'Writing gives [Schulmann] the chance to reflect on the voice's physical vibration, in order to discuss its fragility, emotion, inflections, or its hesitations. On a more fundamental level, the modularity of the voice is understood here as the sign or the symptom of women's condition, a sign whose existence, for a long time, was intentionally ignored. Over the course of the book, *Chicanes*, conceived as a series of fragments, depicts an emotional and intellectual landscape shaped by feminism while allowing the author's own personal journey to show through.'
– *Issue*

'Written in the first person, we find [in *Chicanes*], through a series of fragments, a polyphony of personal situations narrated by voices "thinking out loud". These fragments are mingled with other texts and podcasts, mapping a cartography of thinkers who play out, through the prism of intimacy, the "affective turn" of the social sciences and academic writing in gender studies. As they move away from a linear narrative of technique and knowledge, they leave behind the clear language of rationality experienced in full light and, in its wake, something else is heard like a voice in the night, full of silences, ramblings, hesitations and stutterings.'
– *Zérodeux /02 magazine*

CHICANES

by Clara Schulmann

translated from the French
by Naima Rashid, Natasha Lehrer, Lauren Elkin,
Ruth Diver, Jessica Spivey, Clem Clement,
Jennifer Higgins, and Sophie Lewis

This first English-language edition published by Les Fugitives in the United Kingdom in March 2023 • Les Fugitives Ltd, 91 Cholmley Gardens, Fortune Green Road, West Hampstead, London NW6 1UN • www. lesfugitives.com • Originally published as *Zizanies* © Paraguay Press, 2020 • English-language translation © Naima Rashid, Natasha Lehrer, Lauren Elkin, Ruth Diver, Jessica Spivey, Clem Clement, Jennifer Higgins, and Sophie Lewis, 2023 • Cover design by Sarah Schulte • Typeset in Baskerville and Bookman Old Style by MacGuru Ltd • All rights reserved • No part of this publication may be reproduced, stored in a retrieval system or transmitted in any form or by any means, electronic, mechanical, photocopying, recording or otherwise, without prior permission in writing from Les Fugitives editions • A CIP catalogue record for this book is available from the British Library • The rights of Clara Schulmann to be identified as author, and the rights of N. Rashid, N. Lehrer, L. Elkin, R. Diver, J. Spivey, C. Clement, J. Higgins, and S. Lewis to be identified as respective translators of each section of this work have been identified in accordance with Section 77 of the Copyright, Designs and Patents Act 1988 • Printed in England by CMP, Poole, Dorset • ISBN 978-1-7397783-2-3 •

This book has received support from the French Institute of the United Kingdom as part of the Burgess programme for translation.

CHICANES

LesFugitives

London

In July 2018, I left to spend some days with a friend who lived in the mountains. I had called her a month earlier, confused, because I had just learned that my contract with the art school in Bordeaux, where I was teaching, was not going to be renewed. This news came to me as a brutal blow, and I plodded through the months of May and June in a somewhat haggard state. I took stock of my attachment to this school, where I had spent six years. The students, whose faces and expressions would haunt me for a long time yet, at Parisian street-crossings, at home, and when the endless round trips between Paris and Bordeaux, which had formed the rhythm of my life for so long, came to an end. The vibrant and joyous collective adventure I lived there, where friendships determined what we did and what we wanted to do. It felt like a great big void had suddenly opened up in my life. I consoled myself by saying that it's an opportunity to do things I never got to do, to see people I didn't get to see often enough.

My friend knew that I wasn't feeling very

good, and that this stay at her place was equal parts escape and asylum. During the day, both of us worked on our respective projects. I tried to make progress on the writing that ultimately resulted in this book, while she ran the contemporary art centre in the city, at the foot of the mountains. In the evenings, we chatted while smoking cigarettes. Solenn has worn many hats during her life. One of these was that of a singer. Together, we listened to songs she had written with her then-boyfriend. That was back in 2005, and it seemed like an eternity ago for her. I recorded parts of our conversations on my phone because she has a very literary way of narrating stories; things become clear to her as she says them out loud. When I listen to these recordings again, I hear her present voice speaking over her past voice, the voice of Solenn the singer.

The conversation flowed. We talked about our lives. She told me that at times when she lost her voice, and that happened to her sometimes in moments of intense grief, it was because something she believed in to an unshakeable degree had come crumbling down. She told me that voices create a circuitry between our inner and outer selves, and that's why they are fragile: they are private and domesticated but also public at the same time. This entanglement is sometimes hard to unravel. I told her that this was the very gist of what I was trying to work on.

We also listened to a lot of music together. She showed me the clip of 'Austra', a song by Toronto-based band Beat and the Pulse. All these girls playing together in the band exuded an energy that was both desperate and very decisive. Later, I read an interview with the singer Katie Stelmanis, who said, 'My favourite thing about this video is that it shows a bunch of friends: we hung out, had a great time: it's truly authentic. It's very sexual but not in an objectifying way, it's just a real picture towards female sexuality. It's about girls being them-selves. It felt real and honest. The shooting was very simple and real.'* I felt as if I could tap into these feminine voices, neither wholly soft nor serene, which merged into each other. There is a nervous sort of energy there which resonates with my research. Girls who are singing, who look like they landed from another planet, and who make you want to dance.

This blurry moment in July 2018 revives the actual starting point of this book, a roman-tic break-up that took place more than four

*Katie Stelmanis, 'A Mystery Called Austra', Interview, 29 April 2011, *Electronic Beats*.

years ago. I'm aware of the complete ordinariness of this experience, which so many people have gone through at different points in their lives. The separation in question took place quietly, without any conflict or even a discussion. One fine day, the person with whom I had spent fifteen years of my life was gone. Just like that. He told me he had met someone else. I haven't seen him since. A familiar voice, with which I had conversed all my life, disappeared all of a sudden. This separation imposed the golden rule of silence as a coping mechanism. Up to this point, I had been navigating my way somewhat aimlessly through feminist readings, paying attention to the way one describes one's life, the way one narrates it; these elements are suddenly brought sharply into focus. I track the singular and painful circumstances which make us lose our voices. What I'm living through colours the meaning I read into things. Weaving voices with silence, I move more fluidly through this literature now. It allows me neither to dissect nor to resolve my dilemmas, rather it has another effect; it lends texture to real-life situations by pausing to grant attention to what is sometimes treated in a hurry because, well, 'that's life', or 'it happens', or even still because we don't have the words or the space to talk about these things. I understand the notion that literature gives a certain value to the ordinary, which, seen on its own, is riddled with irregularities.

Since my separation, I have only read, reread or consulted works written by women. I also made a point to listen to several podcasts. Some French programmes (*À voix nue, Transfert, Dans le genre, Les Savantes, Par les temps qui courent*) and also several American podcasts (*Serial, Fresh Air, Stuff Mom Never Told you, The Guilty Feminist, This American Life, Where Should We Begin?*). Stories, interviews, works of fiction and documentaries. I spent my time listening to women speak. I listened to scientists, researchers, journalists, bloggers, actors. I heard women talking about their journeys, their dressing rooms, their doctoral theses, their periods, their illnesses, their children, their fears, their passions, their love affairs, their sexuality. I took notes; a part of them make up this book.

The act of listening without seeing creates some unexpected effects, which are different from those experienced when reading alone. The stories do not imprint themselves on our mind in the same manner; they are filled with tonalities, silences and hesitations. One does not associate them with each other in the same way one does while reading a book. These associations are a lot more fluid and free-flowing, yet chime more easily with real life. Since I used to listen to these podcasts during many of my journeys, especially those between Paris and Bordeaux, I associated their voices with train stations, landscapes in motion and faces on the metro. As a result, they never seemed abstract or disembodied to me, but always anchored in very real situations.

For example, I learned from a radio programme that once women had acquired the right to vote in 1944, their voices became deeper. This 'deepening' of voice goes hand in hand with women's search for recognition, notably in the political and institutional spheres. It is natural to trust a baritone voice more, natural to be more seduced by it. For almost fifty years, voices which were high-pitched and considered characteristically feminine until now, progressively disappeared.

The way we think out loud is at the heart of this book. In this category, I loosely place teaching, interviews, discussions, radio, telephone and psychoanalysis. Even though I grew up in a family where we spoke a lot, sometimes in a very heated manner, the studies I spent so long pursuing have gradually pushed me to favour writing. This situation is quite common. In fact, it's striking in interviews, especially those with theorists: when these women speak, they 'translate' their academic language, a written code, into a common and shared spoken language. One gets to hear the mutations of their voice, the way it becomes charged with emotions or turns cold – inflexions which are never accessible while reading. Our states of tiredness, irritation and joy colour our voices, and this colour goes on to tint our words, pauses and silences. It was when I started teaching seven years ago that these nuances first became apparent to me: the effects, the varying intensities, the clumsiness or the failures of the spoken word, but also its capacity to capture the present. Today, I think of it as a medium which allows one to undo the knowledge of one's position of power and authority by subjecting it to the ordinary climate of everyday life, normal or abnormal, with its hazards, its surprises or, on the contrary, its moroseness.

I remember a poetry initiative which we started in February 2017 in Bordeaux in an art workshop run by myself and three others – the two Benjamins and Armand. The 'love all day marathon', as we called it in our emails, proposed to students to show up that day with 'some songs/poems/writings on love'. We specified further: 'You can bring writings/songs/ books/files that you have written/created or that you can find. We will work together with these writings.' Our idea was to read out loud, to hear our own voices and, possibly, to record each other during readings. Pedagogically, we were convinced that the very act of speaking could stimulate poetic writing. We debated among ourselves how to word the invitation. Finally, Benjamin summed up the activity in an email: 'No more and no less, and that's more than enough. We want serenades, bewitching sonatas, anything you have and anything you know about love.' Basically, a simple announcement and one request: bring a pen and some apples to share. The morning of the day itself, we stopped by the school library to pick up some books which we placed on the table in a small room, number 226, whose windows overlooked the music conservatory.

As far as I remember, our poetry day wasn't a resounding success. Some students made the effort and came to read some pieces with us, but their presence, their attention, and moreover, their participation seemed uncertain. I can't get the idea out of my head that it was the very act of reading aloud which was weighing them down, embarrassing them, as if it exposed them in a peculiar way. That said, by the end of the day, Benjamin and I received an email from Barbara who was never verbose, but who nonetheless came that day to recite some

English poems by Victor Hugo – 'Tomorrow, at dawn'. The email was titled 'poetry stuff' and contained a link to a poem by Edna St-Vincent Millay (1892–1950), an American poet whom I'd never heard of: 'Time does not bring relief; you all have lied/Who told me time would ease me of my pain!/I miss him in the weeping of the rain/I want him at the shrinking of the tide…'*

Teaching remains an experience of delay, or rather a non-convergence of voices; the idea of a result is constantly routed here by this shapeless drifting of days and hours spent together without anything happening in the real sense of the word. To be able to add one's voice to this flow and act as if it still amounts to something is the overarching narrative that one has to succeed in telling oneself. If I was ever able to do it, it was because my voice in Bordeaux was in particularly good company.

The chapters of this book fall naturally into a regular chronicle in which events from my life are placed next to readings, films, stories that were told to me, discussions I was part of, interventions and texts which all fed into this book. Their arrangement in six parts allows

---

* Edna St. Vincent Millay, 'Time Does Not Bring Relief; You All Have Lied', *Renascence and Other Poems*, Harper & Brothers Publishers, 1917.

different spiritual states, 'moments' and tempos to appear. The word 'moment' is grey, dull and relatively vague. This imprecision characterises time that is lived from moment to moment – time which we no longer question because it blends so seamlessly into the everyday. Indefinite but with a cadence at its core, this lived time traps us as much as it sets us free. In the course of a day, or even a single hour, we pass through a lot of different 'moments'. Sometimes, they even overlap. I see them as seasons and cycles which affect our gestures, our bodies and the words we use. We cannot define a moment. We can, however, ask ourselves what is inside it – much like we search the inside a bag.

Around these moments, I have put together an imaginary community of female figures, living and dead, real and fictitious, who, in a way, converse with each other across these pages. The book has been imagined as a listening device where writing serves to record and pre-serve. All one has to do is listen to these voices and isolate them from the contexts in which they initially appeared, so they can be perceived differently. The work takes on the form of a re-transcription, and eventually a reassembling. In drawing up new relationships, the writing gives birth to a new community. It's as if I were trying to conjure into existence an improbable family unseparated by the constraints of time, eras and disciplines.

In a film by director Sophie Fillières, *When Margaux meets Margaux* (2018), two women encounter each other: one is forty years old, the other around twenty-five. The film puts forward an uncanny hypothesis; they are both the same woman, Margaux, at two different points in her life. Sophie Fillières explains: 'We are stratified by the ages we have been in life. Today, I am 50 years old but I'm also simultaneously the person I was when I was 25 and 32 years old. They (the two feminine characters) contain each other as if our selves multiply to contain within our present selves those we have been at past ages and those we are going to become in the future. These selves experience us as we grow and shape us in turn. [...] The question is: how do they blend into each other and tear apart at the same time?'* That is the connection that I research through my examples: putting recordings of people speaking alongside each other, stories rarely linked but which end up becoming ancestors, sisters or great grand-cousins to each other. An eccentric family tree which

---

* Sophie Fillières, '*Comment se rejoindre et se déchirer en même temps ?*', interview by Julien Gester, *Libération*, 13 March 2018.

suggests new connections. While positioning them alongside each other, often clumsily, I decide to preserve them, all the while knowing that it's as much an act of tearing apart as it is one of preserving. I don't always treat these references very well; I cut them up, I rearrange them sometimes, why not, I reinvent them, I throw in quotation marks whenever the fancy takes me. The genealogy I'm drawing up is completely unconcerned with the effects of legitimisation.

The ways in which I can use these stories interests me far more than their exceptional status. I have a friend whose partner, Rosa, worked as a nanny for a chic family in the sixteenth arrondissement of Paris, but she wanted to become a Spanish teacher. On announcing her decision, she left this family. Sadly, her project fell through and she had to take up the job of a nanny again. She found a new family that was looking for a nanny, but they wanted to speak to her previous employer first, to ask how she conducts herself around children, to check her 'references' and so on. She couldn't call the previous family again because she had quit her work saying that she was about to start a new job. My friend called me, asking me to play the role of the family's mother over the phone. I declined – I'm a pathetic actor. In the end, another friend, Lila, agreed to make the phone call and had the following unlikely discussion: she is the mother of a large family who lives in the sixteenth arrondissement, she describes her life, the children's activities, gives details, flatters the person she's speaking to. She took well to this role play, this life she never had and which she invented on the go. As a profession, Lila produces films which borrow from real life, but which resemble fiction in the end. By inserting scripted and performed scenes in the midst of real situations, she looks to create emotions which would be outside the range of documentary projects alone. This mixing up rearranges social relations and recasts them in a different light. Her characters often show combative attitudes and resist being assigned into neat categories. The story with the nanny is interesting because it puts Lila in a situation of writing and role play with which she is familiar, where speech is equal parts fiction and reality, and therefore, takes on a political charge.

In the episode 'The Tape', of the series *Seinfeld*, Elaine, Jerry's BFF, attends one of his performances, sitting at the very back of the room. Next to her, she finds a tape recorder which Jerry has placed there to record his performance in order to listen to it later. On a whim, she launches into an ultra-sensual monologue addressed to Jerry, certain that it will remain anonymous. Jerry discovers the recording the next day. He is captivated by the sweet and languorous voice of this unknown woman. He is determined to find out who she is. He shares the recording with Kramer and George – both of them are equally entranced by the erotic powers of this mysterious voice. Later, under oath of secrecy, Elaine reveals to George that the voice in the recording was hers. Since that moment, George is incapable of simply looking at Elaine in the way that he did before: the fact of having fantasied about this voice and, now, to have to attribute it to someone in the friend zone constitutes an insurmountable dilemma for him.

This discomfort and these manipulations say a lot about the powers of the voice, especially when it becomes dissociated from the body. In the case of *Seinfeld* or the story with the nanny, voice and its attributes, whether real or fictitious, produce effects which spill over into real life. These effects are sometimes so strong that they go on to change the course of real life. As a result, established hierarchies come undone, and new logics sketch themselves into being. The discomfort, the embarrassment or the real solutions produced by these new and unexpected rearrangements point to a simple fact:

our identities never stop being reconfigured; in fact, they are always waiting to become something else. Our voice, in the way it transforms, adapts, tenses up, evades us, signals to us the amplitude of these reconfigurations, of these hidden potentialities. These discords punctuate and nourish our lives.

When I started compiling stories and quotations, I did not know that questions of doubling, of repetition, of mime, of imitation or of masquerade were at the heart of feminist literature. I discovered it later. Donna Haraway addresses the matter well: "'Women's experience" does not pre-exist as a kind of prior resource, ready simply to be appropriated into one or another description. What may count as "women's experience" is structured within multiple and often inharmonious agendas. "Experience", like "consciousness", is an intentional construction, an artefact of the first importance. Experience may also be reconstructed, re-membered, re-articulated. One powerful means to do so is the reading and re-reading of fiction in such a way as to create the effect of having access to another's life and consciousness, whether that other is an individual or a collective person with the lifetime called history. These readings exist in a field of resonating readings, in which each version adds tones and shapes to the others, in both cacophonous and consonant waves.'*

This book brings together these cacophonic sound waves.

Translated by Naima Rashid

---

*Donna J. Haraway, 'Reading Buchi Emecheta: Contests for "Women's Experience" in Women's Studies', in *Simians, Cyborgs, and Women: The Reinvention of Nature*, Routledge.

1. ON/OFF

To be and not to be

Translated by Natasha Lehrer

In 2011 I was hired as an ATER (Temporary Teaching and Research Assistant) in the film department of the University of Lyon 2, on the Bron campus. I was to teach several courses, including a lecture series on 'general aesthetics'. In my memory, the lecture theatre was enormous. To get there I had to go down what seemed like thousands of stairs. I can still picture the students – a row of dark silhouettes sitting quite still behind their computers. I was terrified. I had no idea how to move, how to address those faces, how to look at them. I had no idea how to speak to them either. My voice never managed to adapt to this setup. Given the size of the hall, two solutions presented themselves: either I spoke into the microphone, positioned on the desk at a great distance, almost obliging me to lie across it – and to break my back. Or I gave up on the microphone and relied solely on my own authority. That was what I did. I had the impression that I was incapable of reaching the students unless I spoke extremely loudly, practically shouted. As the weeks went by, my voice stopped working. Not a sound came out of my mouth. I made an appointment in Paris, near Gobelins, with a speech therapist. She taught me how to breathe deep into my abdomen and to stop abusing my vocal cords. I carried on teaching in Lyon until the end of the academic year when I left to go and teach in an art school. It hadn't occurred to me until that point that my voice was going to be my work tool.

///

I started to listen, to really hear voices. The way they can be there and then disappear, the way they reflect our frailties: this discovery made me as sensitive to the pauses and stammerings of voices as to the moments when they flow, when it seems like nothing can stop them. I began to tap into these interruptions, these vocal pauses that are not always intentional.

///

In *Faces in the Crowd* Mexican novelist Valeria Luiselli portrays a writer with two young children. In Mexico, in a house that is slowly falling into ruin, she is trying to write a book. Behind her back, her architect husband reads the pages she has written, surreptitiously keeping an eye on her, while her child pesters her incessantly about what she is doing. She's never left in peace. She's constantly having to stop, put her writing on hold. This interruption is at the heart of the book. The continuous flow that writing demands is irreparably impeded, complicated by things as practical and routine as they are phantasmatic. 'Novels need a sustained breath,' writes the narrator. 'That's what novelists want. No one knows exactly what it means, but they all say: a sustained breath. I have a baby and a boy. They don't let me breathe. Everything I write is – has to be – in short bursts. I'm short of breath.'* Her voice gets lost in the twists and turns of the narrative. Among the themes explored in the novel, I begin to take note of the pauses that she is obliged to establish between herself and her project. I look at how she begins to accept being interrupted. The frustration it engenders, but also how the desire to return to writing surpasses the frustration. I understand that it's the interruption that generates the impulse, the pulse, the expectation, the impatience. As I read on, I noticed how the characters who replace or duplicate the narrator multiply: she

*Valeria Luiselli, *Faces in the Crowd*, translated by Christina MacSweeney, Granta, 2013.

is simultaneously a mother, a young child-
less woman, a writer, an editor in New York, a
translator, but she also steps into the shoes of
the poet she is translating. So when her writing
has to be suspended, we follow her in other
ways, as she invents other lives, other characters, other voices. These identities dissolve into
one another. It occurs to me that the fact of
being constantly interrupted leads to as many
solutions as it does problems.

/ / /

'The most superficial inquiry into women's
writing instantly raises a host of questions'
wrote Virginia Woolf in 'Women and Fiction',
in 1929. 'Why, we ask at once, was there no
continuous writing done by women before the
eighteenth century? Why did they then write
almost as habitually as men, and in the course
of that writing produce, one after another,
some of the classics of English fiction? [...] A
little thought will show us that we were asking
questions to which we shall get, as answer,
only further fiction. The answer lies at present
locked in old diaries, stuffed away in old
drawers, half-obliterated in the memories of the
aged. It is to be found in the lives of the obscure
– in those almost unlit corridors of history

where the figures of generations of women are so dimly, so fitfully perceived. For very little is known about women.'* Unlit corridors, obscure lives, old drawers, private diaries: the voices of women resonating beneath the foundations of the rectilinear, sanctioned routes. From where echoes the irregularity, the peculiar rhythm that switches on and off, escaping the straight, unbroken line. This notion of an irregular rhythm allows me to move away from, even get beyond the idea of failure. Discontinuity, no less than the word, as the condition of writing; this makes me happy. I tell myself: that is how it works for me, too.

/ / /

I think back, for example, to my teaching voice in Bordeaux: this voice turns on and off. I speak and I listen. But I am compelled to speak, even so. I get off the train, say to myself, 'I haven't the faintest idea what I'm going to say to them.' How the words engage, get going, and then shut down, or at least fade, on my return to Paris:

---

*Virginia Woolf, 'Women and Fiction', first published in *Forum* (New York), March 1929, and reprinted in *Essays of Virginia Woolf,* volume 5 (Penguin Books, 2009) ed. Stuart N. Clarke.

my voice returns to being domestic, private, after it's been, let's say, public. I pick up my writing again, solitary; articles to deliver, my work as a critic, so different to teaching, grappling with artistic practice from a completely different perspective. I think a lot about this rhythm, the balance between my 'shared' voice and my writing, whose monastic aspect sometimes seems so much less joyous. I'm even more sensitive to this because students are often very quiet, they're always being asked to speak, to say something, like a plea. When I watch teachers struggling to get them to utter a sound, deep down I envy their right to silence.

///

In 'Visual Pleasure and Narrative Cinema', Laura Mulvey's 1975 foundational feminist essay on Hollywood cinema and its patriarchal structures, the notion of interruption is attributed to female characters: the purpose of their appearance being to interrupt the flow of the narrative. Subjected to the male gaze that intensifies the point of view of the narrative framework, these female characters are suspended in a fragile equilibrium: the continuity of the action needs to be maintained, but their appearance must be erotically satisfying. In dancing and singing set pieces in particular, action, in the strict sense of the term, breaks down. The framing is reconfigured around the female performance, offering the audience a moment of pure contemplation. The interruption is a diversion. Marilyn Monroe in *The River of No Return* (1954), Lauren Bacall in *To Have and Have Not* (1944): when they begin to sing, nothing else matters. Now there is only erotic contemplation, a suspended time where the female voice and body of the showgirl lead the film into an uncertain zone, outside its space-time. Will the story be able to resume where it left off? Is this a straightforward deviation or the very essence of what cinema is seeking to protect?

/ / /

In contrast to these singing voices, intended for contemplation, a pure surface effect that freezes the action, classic cinema offers us some examples of the female voiceover. Inner voices that allow us to hear what's going on inside a woman's head. Joan Bennett's voiceover in Fritz Lang's 1947 film *Secret Beyond the Door* cuts into scenes as a way of bringing the viewer back to the irregular beat of their thoughts. At the beginning of the film the character she plays, Celia, has an unexpected encounter in Mexico with her future husband. Sitting in a bar, the two characters speak for the first time. He's bewitched by her. He tells her what he sees in her, what her face makes him think of: the calm before the storm. A torrent of words filled with images, cyclones and thunder. In the midst of this meteorological peroration, Celia's voiceover interrupts, speaking over his words as he carries on speaking: 'I heard his voice and then I didn't hear it anymore. Because the beating of my blood was louder. [...] And for an endless moment I seemed to float. Like a feather blown to a place where time had stopped.' Charmed but headstrong, Celia hears something different to the grandiloquent speech of her companion. She is articulating the rhythm of her heart. Throughout the film this voiceover returns, a way of marking the convergence of the young woman's deepest thoughts. A camouflaged beat. The voiceover produces variants and hypotheses, some more fruitful than others, new associations that challenge the narrative of the images. The character frees herself from the grip of the 'scene,' allowing an inner narrative of unusual scope to be heard. Bennett's voiceover in *Secret Beyond the Door* entwines affect, breathing, and a woman's murmured thoughts in a way rarely encountered in the cinema of that era.

///

Women's voices, because of the irregularity of their appearances, are apprehended in different tempos, at different speeds. They grab, hold on, break the flow. But this interplay of switching on and off also exposes an anxiety: What to say? How to say it? Speaking reveals inadequacy, silence, solitude, hesitation.

///

'That spring,' writes Deborah Levy in the first volume of her 'living autobiography', 'when life was very hard and I was at war with my lot and simply couldn't see where there was to get to, I seemed to cry most on escalators at train stations. Going down them was fine but there was something about standing still and being carried upwards that did it. From apparently nowhere tears poured out of me and by the time I got to the top and felt the wind rushing in, it took all my effort to stop myself from sobbing. It was as if the upward movement of the escalator carrying me forwards and upwards was a physical expression of a conversation I was having with myself. Escalators, which in the early days of their invention were known as "travelling staircases" or "magic stairways", had mysteriously become danger zones.'*

///

In my therapist's waiting room, it's mostly women sitting with their coffees, their phones, their laptops, their books, or writing intently in their notebooks as they wait. The wait can be a long one. They glance around, a few hold muttered conversations, mostly they stare into space. The atmosphere is welcoming, even if we mostly tend to sit in silence. I think of us as athletes: concentrated, focused, hushed, on the starting block, gathering ourselves to speak the moment we walk through the door of the consulting room. Sometimes a grey cat joins us. He stretches out along the radiator and contemplates us, as though wondering what on earth all these women are doing there.

///

Since *Les Goddesses* (2011), the artist Moyra Davey has employed an unusual technique in films such as *Notes on Blue* (2015): she writes and

---

*Deborah Levy, *Things I Don't Want to Know*, London: Penguin Books, 2013.

prerecords the voiceover, which she then plays back during filming, listening to her own words through an earpiece connected to the mobile phone she holds in her hand. She explains that before she started using this method, she would try to memorise the entire text. It took her three years to complete her first film. Too laborious. So it was first and foremost a practical choice that meant she didn't have to learn too much material by heart. Then she came to like it: the result was strange, ambiguous, gripping. She began to appreciate the acrobatic aspect of the enterprise, the way she would regularly stumble over the words (her own) spoken in her own voice, make mistakes, start again from the beginning. Davey's films trace a steep trajectory. The scripts combine things she's read, films, memories, different eras, journeys – often without transition. The sound of her voice – always very focused and composed, though she often makes mistakes – prevents a fluid visualisation of her films. Barricaded inside her apartment that is also her studio, her control tower, the artist anxiously paces up and down. Her work is tantamount to a recital, a slightly dizzying, active rehearsal, in which she repeatedly plays herself. I'm particularly interested in the way she uses her voice, the technique she has of seeming to flaunt and celebrate failure.

/ / /

As a teenager I watched the 1994 film *Reality Bites* over and over again. It opens with Winona Ryder's clear, distinctive voice, backed by a faint echo. At first, as the credits appear against a blue background, the viewer doesn't know where the voice is coming from. Images, filmed with a handheld camera, appear onscreen. We see a group of friends dressed for graduation. They wave at the camera. At the same time, the names of the actors appear on screen. The scene shifts to a crowded stadium. Out of this sea of anonymous faces, the camera picks out the girl whose voice we are listening to: 'And they wonder why those of us in our twenties refuse to work an 80-hour week... just so we can afford to buy their BMWs... why we aren't interested... in the counterculture that they invented... if we did not see them disembowel their revolution... for a pair of running shoes. But the question remains... what are we going to do now? How can we repair all the damage we inherited? Fellow graduates, the answer is simple. The answer is... The answer is... I don't know.' The title of the film, *Reality Bites,* appears over the face of Winona Ryder in a tasselled mortarboard. She's rifling through her notes for the answer to the question she's chosen to ask in this highly symbolic graduation speech. We realise she's mislaid the page, that the question is going to remain unanswered. Still, she gets a round of applause. She smiles, embarrassed. Music strikes up. In the next scene we see her with her friends, they're all wasted, eating pizza on the rooftop of an apartment building. Still the same wobbly handheld camera (it's hers – she's making a documentary about their lives, and everyone will get their turn to hold the camera in the film). So the film opens with university graduation, on the cusp of the great leap into the beginning of 'real life'. The uncertainty that interrupted the heroine's graduation speech becomes the obsessive focus of the images shot by the young woman in the course of the film.

/ / /

In her 2006 book, *Death 24x a Second: Stillness and the Moving Image,* Laura Mulvey explores the technology of what she calls the 'delayed', the ability to slow down film, which the introduction of the DVD during the domestic reign of our relationship with cinema made possible for all. Details that had hitherto lain dormant, waiting to be revealed, we could now see thanks to our newfound ability to slow down and freeze the frame. A different relationship to film was born.

Mulvey uncovers a sort of ambivalence, impurity, uncertainty, displacing traditional oppositions. This effect, what Mulvey calls 'delaying cinema', is related to intermittent, specifically female, appearances and disappearances.

/ / /

For a few weeks I immersed myself in a genre of American literature known as 'Quit-Lit': texts that tell stories of giving up work, taking unexpected leave, interruption. Against the background of American academia (the portrait of which it paints is truly horrifying) it's a genre of writing that gathers together those who can no longer cope, who are no longer productive, who give up jobs and promises of promotion. The consequent interruption is genuine, and the suffering is too. It forces us to reject 'deliverology' – the requirement to furnish results. In her essay, 'On Quitting', sociologist Francesca Coin writes: 'In this sense quitting can be understood as a process of rebellion and self-preservation. Subjectivity is no longer defined by the values of neoliberalism: it unveils a certain loyalty to different values and principles. For more and more academics, the inner dislocation between their inner longing and their obligations finds resolution in an audacity that leads them to choose the risk of unemployment over the betrayal of dignity. In this case, quitting is also a way to find one's own voice.'* I'm fascinated by these accounts. I sense they are articulating something that's rarely talked about, particularly in the academic world: the desire to do something else, to start afresh. Lots of my friends talk about their desire to quit, but I don't know anyone who's actually done it. I wonder how these alternative lives are constructed – other than in our heads, I mean.

/ / /

We invited the poet Lisa Robertson to Bordeaux to lead a workshop. During the introductory session she explained that in order to write and publish, we must begin where we are; often we are far too harsh in judging this place, even though it's the site of our daily lives, the place from which our raw material is drawn. She talked about insecurity and seeking kindness in our relationship with writing and reading. I don't know how the students received it, but for me her words were salutary. It was Lisa who introduced me to the work of Denise Riley, the

---

*Francesca Coin, 'On Quitting', in *ephemera journal*: Theory & Politics in Organization, 'The Labour of Academia', volume 17 (3).

English philosopher, poet and feminist, born in 1948. In 1988 Riley published a polemical essay, *Am I That Name? Feminism and the Category of 'Women' in History,* in which she explores with great sensitivity the zone of indecision that she believes exemplifies the category of 'woman'. Her inquiry turns on three main questions: 'When am I a woman?', 'What do "women" mean, and when?', and 'What can "women" do?' She acknowledges that the difficulty in identifying the characteristics of 'women' can engender a certain anxiety. Yet this is precisely the power of the text – her acceptance of the lack of clarity. 'Equality; difference; "different but equal" – the history of feminism since the 1790s has zigzagged and curved through these incomplete oppositions upon which it is itself precariously erected. This swaying motion need not be a wonder, nor a cause for despair. If feminism is the voicing of "women" from the side of "women", then it cannot but act out the full ambiguities of that category. This reflection reduces some of the sting and mystery of feminism's ceaseless oscillations, and allows us to prophesy its next incarnations.'* Lisa and Denise's words become

---

*Denise Riley, *Am I That Name? Feminism and the Category of 'Women' in History*, Minneapolis: University of Minnesota Press, 1988.

conflated in my mind: a woman's everyday life could be the starting point for all the things that absorb her. This in no way simplifies either her everyday life, or the fact of being a woman.

/ / /

Sometimes identities themselves disrupt, hesitate, shift from one regime – one gender – to another, go back to where they started. This back and forth can be laborious or the opposite, effortless. It manifests in granular detail the textures and habits that can change without one even noticing. Specific activities might guide us towards certain gestures, clothes and reflexes that eventually become indispensable. This was how the director Jill (now Joey) Soloway put it in a 2014 conversation with Terry Gross about their television series, *Transparent*, a comedy drama about a Los Angeles family discovering that their parent is a trans woman called Maura. Gross, a superb interviewer, presents the radio show, *Fresh Air*, and her voice has captivated listeners for decades. Her interviewees always give the impression of knowing her well, and the familiarity that results gives the show its unusual charge. I listened to Gross interviewing Soloway on one of my endless train journeys. Soloway talked about the different

ways they have dressed over the years and what
their clothes express about their uncertainties:
'Today I would say I'm dressed sort of like a
boy. And on other days I look pretty feminine
and will put on makeup and get my hair done
and look pretty ladylike. And I think I've always
had that struggle my whole life of feeling a little
bit more gender-neutral, feeling more comfortable as a creative person when I'm dressed like
a boy, when I'm dressed more masculine. So if
I'm doing comedy, if I'm writing, if I'm working,
I really like to be, like, in a – I like to wear jeans
and a T-shirt and no makeup and feel kind of
masculine because it makes me really focus
on what I'm doing. And it puts the work first,
which is odd to even say that, to even realize
that little codes and cues like I don't need to
be looked at, I don't need to be appreciated, I
don't need to be pretty, allow me to be more
creative. I mean, just that sentence is totally
fascinating and I'm only realizing it right now.
But then when I have to be photographed or I
have to be seen or, you know, Jill Soloway the
showrunner, go on stage, get my picture taken,
I really, really don't like the way I look. I mean,
I have to put on – I have to get my hair and my
makeup done or I look when I'm photographed
like somebody I don't want to look like, which
is this really weird struggle. So I, you know, as

a woman, as a feminist, I constantly struggle with how femme do I want to look? How pretty do I need to be? What makes me feel the most comfortable? I struggle with it every day. Every morning I have to ask myself, you know, how am I going to dress to get out of the house? And I remember, you know, a few years ago, before my parent came out actually, like, crying before an HBO Emmy party because I was wearing clothes that I hated, but I felt like I had to wear to dress up. So whatever it is – Spanx, pantyhose, bra – you know, like, all that stuff that means lady dressed up. If I'm not in the right mood, it can make me just start sobbing. And I know a lot of women who feel that way, like that they feel that they're putting on drag when they're getting quote, unquote "dressed up".'*

/ / /

These voices deploy capacities of adjustment that factor in this idea of proceeding in fits and starts. The women in this first group I've written about actively integrate hesitation, failure, even sometimes their desire to disappear. For them, there have been more chicanes than straight roads.

---

* 'Funny, Dirty, Sad: The "Holy Trinity" for "Transparent" Creator Jill Soloway,' *Fresh Air*, 30 October 2014.

///

These adjustments are exciting when they become conscious ways of living and working, when the deviations become stories in their own right, always with the aim of bringing down the patriarchal authority that lurks not far away. So it's only women who can bring about such circumventions, such situations of deferral. And only women who can narrate them. In a 2010 interview, the philosopher, Avital Ronell, describes how she writes and works: 'I think I have a rapport with things that haunt authority, even when it's a paltry authority, underexamined, and these things have no legitimacy, power, or potency. I tend towards things that suggest weakness, rather than a kind of virile muscularity. I adapt my procedures to the object that interests me, I say to myself, for example: "Here, I'm going to be a detective; there's been a crime, there are mysteries and clues." To give myself courage, I adopt a role; sometimes I'm the ghost's secretary, I stand there chewing gum, thinking about something else, wondering what time I can leave, and at the same time I'm listening, I take dictation, which is a way of submitting to authority, even though at the same time I'm not interested, I'm not paid enough to put up with this. This disinterestedness is a pose that helps me to stay close to what's there in the background.'*

///

In a passage in her 1985 book, *My Emily Dickinson* Susan Howe counters 'confident masculine voices' with the notion of a singularly female hesitation, like a paradoxical driving force: 'HESITATE, from the Latin, meaning to stick. Stammer. To hold back in doubt, have difficulty speaking.'[†] So the hesitation comes from speech, orality. Is there a way to hesitate in writing?

///

'That "women" is indeterminate and impossible is no cause for lament,' writes Denise Riley towards the end of *Am I That Name? Feminism and the Category of 'Women' in History*. 'It is what makes feminism; which has hardly been an indiscriminate embrace anyway of the fragilities and peculiarities of the category. What these do demand is a willingness, at times,

---

*Jérôme Lèbre, Laure Vermeersch and Lise Wajeman, 'Qui est à l'appareil ? Entretien avec Avital Ronell,' *Vacarme* no 53, 8 November 2010.
† Susan Howe, *My Emily Dickinson,* Berkeley, California: North Atlantic Books, 1985.

to shred this 'women' to bits – to develop a speed, a foxiness, versatility. The temporalities of 'women' are like the missing middle term of Aristotelian logic; while it's impossible to thoroughly be a woman, it's also impossible never to be one. On such shifting sands feminism must stand and sway.'* The themes of interruption, of fits and starts, switching on and off, obscure the notion that events, feelings, definitions are often layered over each other.

///

In November 2014 I sent an email to some women friends asking for help with packing up the apartment I was moving out of. It had been a couple of months since I'd slept there. They came over with my sisters one Saturday and went through everything, dividing it all up. In a whirlwind of activity, they'd point to things, clothes, kitchen stuff. Even though I was collapsed in a heap on the sofa, I'd say, 'That's mine, that's his'. Sometimes I didn't dare claim something, and so they'd decide for me. At around the same time, I met an Italian man at the Pompidou Centre, who shook my hand with immense seriousness as he introduced himself.

---

*Denise Riley, *op.cit.*

His name was Enrico. We went for a drink one evening. On my way to meet him I popped into the apartment, which was filled with boxes and plunged into darkness. I just wanted to clear the corridor quickly. I was wearing headphones. A song came on and I found myself dancing on my own among the packing crates. It turns out it's not always possible to clear things out. Life muddles things up, piles up moments and voices.

'The idea of singing for you already makes me blush with fear before I even start, but on top of that, to ensure my pronunciation is clear! As if that were nothing! At most, I can produce a sound if I don't have to worry about the diction. And what about you, do you really articulate the words so clearly?

In truth, you have no idea how rusty my voice is; for the past two years I have barely sung at all.'

Clara Schumann
Letter to Robert, 22 March 1840

2. BREATHING

Avoiding death

Translated by Lauren Elkin

I don't breathe enough, allowing only the bare minimum of air to trickle in, just a tiny little bit – frugal, tight, barely ventilating my body. According to my *kiné*, what I do can barely be called 'breathing.' Most of the time I am in a total state of apnea. My stomach, my thorax, my chest all freeze up. They are expecting *air*, which when it arrives only manages to nourish a negligible part of each of them. Entire regions of my body are insufficiently oxygenated. Leave it to me to be stingy about something that's free and available whenever I want. I am convinced that this restriction impacts everything else in my life. In seeking out that which constrains or supports the breath, I believe I will come to think about the voice in a different way – what feeds it, or, on the contrary, what deprives it. I am interested in the quality of air contained in the objects and voices I gather together.

/ / /

At Solenn's place in the mountains, I take pho-
tographs with my phone of her naturopath's
recommendations for breathing. It seems we can
survive 40 to 75 days maximum without eating,
4 to 7 days tops without drinking, and only
4 to 5 minutes without breathing. I make my
mind up to change my habits, and I download
a stress management app called Respirelax on
my phone. A little air bubble floats up and back
down to indicate when to inhale and exhale.

///

In 1848, in a letter, Charlotte Brontë provides
an assessment of *Pride and Prejudice*, by Jane
Austen, published thirty years earlier. She
describes the novel as 'a carefully fenced, highly
cultivated garden, with neat borders and delicate
flowers: but no glance of a bright, vivid physiog-
nomy, no open country, no fresh air, no blue
hill, no bonny beck. I should hardly like to live
with her ladies and gentlemen, in their elegant
but confined houses.'* In short, she finds the
novel stifling: lacking air, breath, breadth.

---

* Sonjung Cho, *An Ethics of Becoming: Configurations of
Feminine Subjectivity in Jane Austen, Charlotte Brontë
and George Eliot*, Routledge, New York, 2006.

///

One year in Bordeaux I proposed a course called 'Catching our Breath.' For the last class I excerpted a sequence from James Cameron's film *Abyss* (1989). It's the part where the couple played by Ed Harris and Mary Elizabeth Mastrantonio are stuck in a tiny submarine at the bottom of the sea, which is slowly taking on water. The water is icy. She sees only one solution: she is going to voluntarily drown herself, submit to hypothermia. She says her body is going to slow down, that it's not going to stop. He is the stronger swimmer, he will put on the only diving suit they have and bring her body up to the oil platform where the rest of the team is waiting, and resuscitate her. Like the rest of the film, the scene is bathed in swimming pool blue. The young woman is finally brought back from the dead after an anguished scene in which a completely distraught Ed Harris shouts at her 'Breathe!' and 'Fight!'

///

In an essay on Zelda Fitzgerald, the writer Elizabeth Hardwick transcribes something Scott wrote. We hear him complain about her, the way he thinks she's too dependent on him. She lives, he says, 'under a greenhouse which is my money and my name and my love. [...] She is willing to use the greenhouse to protect her in every way, to nourish every sprout of talent and to exhibit it – and at the same time she feels no responsibility about the greenhouse and feels she can reach up and knock a piece of glass out of the roof any moment, yet she is shrewd enough to cringe when I open the door of the greenhouse and tell her to behave or go.'* The citation, the violence of this masculine authority exerting itself with such tranquil assurance, stays in my mind for a long time. I think of Zelda trapped in the greenhouse: preserved, suffocating. I begin to link femininity with confinement and discursive powerlessness. The greenhouse offers me a way to think about the circulation of air – the good kinds, and the bad.

/ / /

---

* Elizabeth Hardwick, *Seduction and Betrayal* (1970). New York: NYRB Classics, 2001. [Translator's note: the French word for greenhouse and conservatory is 'serre', which also refers to a 'closed space in which something is preserved,' as well as the words for lock, pressing (as in wine or oil), handshake, and a bird's talon. Schulmann plays on these multiple meanings for containment or pressure in what follows, and I have tried to preserve the ambiguity of the French *serre* wherever possible.]

At the centre of Manet's painting *In the Conservatory* (1879) a woman poses: corseted, gloved, a belt cinching her waist, a bracelet manacling her wrist. She sits on a bench, and stares out in front of her. Vegetation invades the space around her. She is contained by and in the image, but also in a state of total reverie, her gaze undefined. Women and plants – both mute. The vases and flowerpots maintain this feeling of enclosure. They are the instruments of domesticity – laughably insufficient, it has to be said, in the face of all this proliferating plant-life which threatens to obscure the figures. This impression of compression also colours the silence that reigns over the scene, the impossibility of exchange between the man and the young woman towards whom he leans.

/ / /

In September 2014, Thomas and I offered a research program for our masters students, called 'Modern Lovers.' Our initial attempts to describe the project were vague: *we want to talk about feelings, about the importance of collaboration, about affective relationships, about atmospheres*. We were also wondering how to let some air into our teaching – the school had been through a turbulent time, we had suffered disappointment, we no longer knew what was even worthwhile to talk about. We felt we had to open the school up a bit, that otherwise everything we did, or wanted to do, all of our projects would suffer from the pressure, and that we would suffocate. We worked on *Modern Lovers* for three years. Our initial conversations were dominated by weather-related vocabulary: we used the word *breeze* a lot. This research seminar offers this hypothesis: in a time characterised by a form of depression – political and social depression no doubt, but depression in the field of art, perhaps, as well – the lexicon of "climate" helps us define new critical and artistic positions and attitudes, and to conceive of different ways of organising ourselves, a modern micropolitics. "Disturbances," "feelings, "atmosphere," "temperature," "mood": these terms reveal a paradoxical and previously unseen dynamic which situates the most vital and important things in the natural world, which is (by nature) diffuse and imprecise [...] What is really at stake in this project? To follow a feeling: this renewal (semantic, critical, methodological), in attempting to climatically understand the contemporary situation, may help us to think in new ways about the gaps between individual destinies and collective projects and commitments. Attending to the way air circulates between the studio, the outdoors, the gallery, journals, and music, will allow us to dismantle the field of art, to challenge its individualist aims and to invest above all in a distribution of the sensible, and the pooling of resources.' We were delighted with our project. It allowed us to group together lectures, films, ideas, and, especially, lived experience. After the first year, when we tried to hold a regular seminar, with guests, presentations, discussions – which were met with little enthusiasm – we decided the following year to set the project in some faraway geographical location where it could thrive. We picked Athens because Greece was at that time at the centre of every conversation, because documenta* was going to be held there, and because we had the impression that it was a place where something was happening, where we could breathe a different air.

/ / /

---

*documenta is considered the largest contemporary art event in the world. It takes place every five years. In 2017, exceptionally, the organisers decided to hold it jointly in Kassel, its usual site, and in Athens, which was at the time undergoing an unprecedented economic, social and political crisis.

I'm looking at the Manet painting because I'm writing a piece about a film by a Malaysian director called Tan Chui Miu, *A Tree in Tanjung Malim* (2004). A young woman returns to what we imagine to be her hometown looking for a man who is older than her. They spend a night together. They talk a little, they sing, they walk around, they look at apartments lit up in the night. The idea of this couple that wasn't really a couple led me to the painting, because of the somewhat veiled seduction that threads through the film and its heavy, discomfiting silences. The young woman is about to turn eighteen, and at the very end of the film the male character (in the credits he is called the 'beautiful loser') gives her a copy of George Eliot's *Middlemarch*. In my essay, I completely neglected to talk about this gift and its significance. I hadn't yet read *Middlemarch*, though I have since. The novel is set in a small provincial town in early nineteenth-century England. Several women's destinies collide there. Each tries to follow her intuition, to open the right window in a world that seems terribly restrictive. The novel makes room for the idea of failure, of the wrong choice – especially in the case of marriage. Several characters make mistakes. The unions to which they consent or to which they aspire are based on profound misunderstandings. In Tan Chui Mui's film, the characters try to be together, to be a couple, but in spite of their desire, something insurmountable gets in their way. And so the film is something like a missed encounter, in which the silences are particularly perceptible because they carry within them all the characters' disappointments. 'It's my misfortune to have met you,' says the loser towards the end of the film. 'The misfortune is all mine,' the young woman responds.

///

Then there is that scene in *Gone with the Wind* (1939) in which Scarlett, who has just had a baby, holds tight to a bedpost and asks Mammy to lace up her corset even tighter, because she believes herself to be as fat (20 inches) as Aunt Pitty. She wants to get back to the 18 and a half inches her waist used to measure. Mammy has to explain to her that she will never be that size again: 'It ain't nothing to do about it.' I look at the conversion tables. In 2019, the smallest waist (XXS) begins at 24 inches (59/63 cm). Scarlett's waist, before and after her pregnancy, no longer exists.

///

I wonder what women who wear corsets do about breathing. I gather images from literature, from painting, or film in which women are on display, preserved – embalmed, almost, by the apparatuses that encircle them (the greenhouse, the corset – different ways of being contained). But: it is clear that these apparatuses are permanently deviant. When I look into the effects of breathing, and the function of the breath, I understand how these diversions are created, which paths they take.

/ / /

Edith Wharton's writing demands that we decipher and interpret signs: 'A kind of hieroglyphic world' unfolds before us in *The Age of Innocence* (1920), where flowers and plants are associated with feminine figures, with their silence, and their decorative presence, which proves to be what holds together a society completely frozen by convention. When Martin Scorcese adapted it for the cinema in 1993, he hired Elaine and Saul Bass to design the opening credits. Flowers bloom against a black background, layered over with images of lace and handwriting. The film's literary provenance is immediately feminised. But the flowers begin to unfurl more quickly, revealing their pistils like half-told secrets, invading the screen, slowly becoming romantic and more unsettling. The ritual, the rhythm, the hidden, enslaving constraint: the New York life depicted in the book and the film rarely gave buds enough time to blossom. The greenhouses and winter gardens that make up its interiors give more importance to artifice than to the natural progression of flowers. There is something of the naturalist about Wharton, or the botanist; the inevitable wilting (of flowers, plants or women) remains the constant horizon against which she deploys the different artifices of conservation.

/ / /

Invited to speak at a conference in Paris, I try to gather my thoughts about greenhouses, plants, voices and silence. By way of an introduction I begin with a verse from a poem by Mathilde Wesendonck (who was married to one of Wagner's benefactors, and with whom he was very much in love), 'Im Treibhaus' (In the Greenhouse, 1858). The poem is part of the 'Wesendonck Lieder,' written for a female voice and solo piano – and I've read that it's the one time that Wagner agreed to set music to texts that he himself had not written. It's addressed to some plants:

Children of far-off places
Tell me why you lament.
In silence you tend your branches,
And trace signs in the air,
And in mute witness to your sorrow,
A sweet perfume arises.*

My talk brought together films, texts, an image
of a self-portrait by Lee Krasner next to a plant
(*Self-Portrait*, 1929) looking at the viewer, a
poem by Katherine Mansfield, and photos of
Edith Wharton in the garden of her country
estate, the Pavillon Colombe, in 1935. I describe
the slightly stiff, muddy atmosphere of the
greenhouse, where women are often to be found
nearby. When I brought these materials together
again for a seminar with my Bordeaux students,
I added a scene from *Minority Report* (2002), the
Steven Spielberg film in which Tom Cruise's
character, John Anderton, questions one of
the founders of a company called Precrime, Iris
Hineman, an older woman who receives him in

---

* Mathilde Wesendonck, 'Im Treibhaus' (In the
Greenhouse), third song in the *Wesendonck Leider*
composed by Richard Wagner between 1857 and 1858
and published in 1862 under the title Five Poems for
Female Voice with Piano Accompaniment – though the
name of the song's female author was unmentioned.
Translation mine (such as it is).

a lush luxuriant greenhouse, full of carnivorous plants. She confirms that among the three precogs who can predict the future, there is one who sometimes disagrees with the others; she tells him this embarrassing 'minority report' must be found and destroyed. But how, he asks, will he know which one it is? It will be the more gifted of the three, she tells him. 'The female.'

/ / /

Now, I am a plant, a weed,
Bending and swinging
On a rocky ledge
And now I am a long brown grass
Fluttering like flame
I am a reed;
An old shell singing
For ever the same
A drift of sedge
A white, white stone
A bone
Until I pass
Into sand again,
And spin and blow
To and fro, to and fro,
On the edge of the sea
In the fading light...
For the light fades.

But if you were to come you would not say
She is not waiting here for me
She has forgotten. Have we not in play
Disguised ourselves as weed and stones and
    grass
While the strange ships did pass
Gently – gravely – leaving a curl of foam
That uncurled softly about our island home
Bubbles of foam that glittered on the stone
Like rainbows. Look, darling! No they are
    gone.
And the white sails have melted into the
    sailing sky...*

///

In *Daniel Deronda,* George Eliot's last novel, Gwendolen doesn't understand until the night before her tragic marriage the extent to which her choices do not belong to her. Until that moment, she had been living in a state of innocence, in which she believed herself to be in charge of her life. Very slowly, she begins to perceive the restraints tightening gently around her. In an exchange with her future husband, she tries to

---

*Katherine Mansfield, 'Now I am a plant, a weed.'
Poems of Katherine Mansfield. Auckland: Oxford UP, 1988.

explain what she's feeling: "'We women can't go in search of adventures – to find out the North-West Passage or the source of the Nile, or to hunt tigers in the East. We must stay where we grow, or where the gardeners like to transplant us. We are brought up like the flowers, to look as pretty as we can, and be dull without complaining. That is my notion about the plants; they are often bored, and that is the reason why some of them have got poisonous. What do you think?" Gwendolen had run on rather nervously, lightly whipping the rhododendron bush in front of her.'*

///

In 2015, the writer, poet and critic Quinn Latimer wrote an essay about her mother that she called 'My Mother, My Other: or, Some Sort of Influence.' The same year, I conducted a series of interviews for the Jeu de Paume's online magazine, which focused on artists with a double practice: film and writing. I called it 'Emotional Technologies', and Quinn, along with a little less than 20 other artists, agreed to answer my questions. The last one read: 'Writing, like film,

---

*George Eliot, *Daniel Deronda* (1876). London: Penguin Classics, 1995.

calls upon or resuscitates ghosts. Who or what haunts you?' She replied: 'My mother.' In her essay, she describes her vital relationship to reading and to books, and to the almost exclusively feminine references transmitted to her by her mother: 'I suppose I had been doing it my whole life: reading the books my mother read, watching the films she watched, trying on the politics she wore, sometimes embodied. Feeling her sensibilities cross my face. What that felt like. Trying on her intelligence, her seriousness, her ambition, wit, anger, grief, skepticism, mania, ardor. It was a look. And while moving through those looks, those books [...] I began recognizing in the pages of these critical and literary women a gravity that my mother had herself gleaned and adopted, tried and taken on. [...] A look with a lineage not just familial or genetic. Something else.'* Her mother had been a compulsive reader, bringing her children up on her own, running one bookshop after another on the West Coast of the US, bipolar, alcoholic, getting work where she could, but always surrounded by books. Quinn read in her mother's footsteps, the same books, the same dogeared

---

* Quinn Latimer, 'My Mother, My Other: or, Some Sort of Influence' (2015), in *Like a Woman: Essays, Readings, Poems*. Berlin: Sternberg Press, 2017.

pages – through which influences and language transmitted themselves. She writes that she is trying to find a 'genetic model': a genealogy, a possible origin – she calls this a *'rivering'* question: it's a river, a flow, a flux. 'The rivering question of the literary daughter.' Quinn's text thus poses the question of the model, that which we imitate, which we follow, which constrains us, and which also opens new paths. Can we breathe in someone else's footsteps. The question of breath opens for me that of descent [*filiation*], in the sense of invisible threads [fils, *threads* but also *sons*] woven between books, which create internal draughts [*appels d'air*].

/ / /

I'm wondering how to mark off silences, particularly in transcribing an interview or a conversation. Pauses and hesitations occur frequently, and I tend to erase them, as if they had never existed. The journalist and writer Sheila Heti worked for several years as the interviews editor for the culture magazine *The Believer*. In May 2018, on a podcast called *Longform* on which writers discuss their work habits, she describes the way she thought of these interviews: like plays, with a kind of narrative arc extending over several acts, pauses and sections – putting aside the more natural flow of a conversation. Interviews sometimes need to be rewritten, revised, cleaned-up, while remaining as close as possible to what the person interviewed thinks or says. In 2013, Heti interviewed the writer and critic Chris Kraus, when her novel *Summer of Hate* was published. I'll cite a section from their conversation on women's silence and the supposed enigmas it hides:

> Chris Kraus: [...] I've noticed among younger people in the art world the white male thing that's just very smart and very cold. Very cold. It's total affect, right? Hiding something else. So you get tired of that, right? In one's own life, you get tired of that. And you just want to be with people who are more or less who they are at face value.
>
> BLVR: Women used to have something similar, no? There was the woman who was very silent and didn't speak and had this mystery that men would fall for because they would project onto her. I don't see that there's a lot of women like that anymore.
>
> CK: No.
>
> BLVR: But were there?
>
> CK: Women who could remain just

completely silent? Well, yeah, but it had to be combined with a tremendous physical beauty. And glamour, you know? It couldn't be a pockmarked, craggy girl who just doesn't talk. [Laughs]

BLVR: Do you see that in the young art girls? The beauty and the emptiness?

CK: No. Not the ones that I meet. The ones that I meet are incredibly open and, you know, alive and forthcoming.*

///

A friend told me the impression it made on her to hear her shrink's voice when, asking to be buzzed into his building, it came through the intercom saying, invariably, 'I'll let you in.'

///

And so about fifteen or so students from the Bordeaux school went to work in Athens for six months. We found them internships in different places, some related to the art world, some not; they had a stipend to live on, and housing, and they regularly sent back news.

---

* Sheila Heti, 'An Interview with Chris Kraus,' *The Believer*, 1 September 2013, n°101.

Thomas and I spent time there in April 2017. We organised a number of events with artists, performances and studio visits, but the trip was, above all, regularly punctuated with conversations about these 'air currents' which so obsessed us. In Athens, we find answers to our need for a change of scene – it wasn't as easy to sidestep certain complexities and uncertainties as it was at home. I have a particularly intense memory of our having conversations about the presidential elections which were approaching in France at that time: questions about politics crept in everywhere we turned. Among the people we met with in Athens was the artist Georgia Sagri, who led a workshop in the neighborhood of Kerameikos, in a studio which someone had lent us for the occasion. She sits us in a circle on rugs, or on the blankets she'd asked us to bring with us. The circle is large that day; a number of students have come along. The workshop consists of learning to breathe. Georgia shows us exercises she knows very well – she calls it a 'training,' a 'score', like in music – something she has practised on her own for a little over a decade. This training is also at the heart of the performance she was doing at documenta. She called it *Dynamis*, and explained in an interview, 'Most of the time, we're trying to adapt to something

that we see, and we try to mimic, and the better
we do this, the more we form our bodies and
qualities. But each person has their own conditions and their own capacities to exist and
experience everything, so I understand training as a way to abandon this idea of mastery
– mimicking someone – in order to acquire and
understand the unique qualities that each of
us carry; that is, in my opinion, taking care of
the self. Which for me at least is also the base,
the foundation, for the medium of performance.
Or any kind of medium of using the body as
primal material.'* Seated in a circle, we began
to count, and our breathing progressively took
on a rhythm. An inhale, and then an exhale,
long, or not. Slowly we add in gestures. Georgia
comes around behind us, making corrections,
or slipping into the centre of the circle to give us
instructions. Her voice – which could be direct,
even cutting – lends structure to the day-long
session. She explains that if we could understand how to breathe correctly, we'd learn 'how
to fall, and not get hurt.' Breath is a tool which
can make us hardier. Breathing is the result of
a decision, Georgia tells us, but what she also
tells us is that without breath or air, we are

* Georgia Sagri interviewed by Ross Simonini,
ArtReview, December 2017.

that much more permeable to our fear and our disquiet.

///

The artist Tacita Dean wrote an essay on the painter Cy Twombly in which she mentions his obsession with ancient Greece. She recounts a memory: a voyage to Delphi on a university exchange program when she was 22 years old. Alone on the mountain, she sensed a storm approaching. She saw the sky change, the birds grow fretful; the wind began to blow. Hiding under a rock, she experienced an immense, panicked fear. She came to Twombly through the intervention of Pan, one of the ancient deities fetishised by the painter. 'Pan is the horned and hairy half-goat god of nature who embodies the spirit of the landscape and the excitement that it inspires in us. The feeling of alarm one gets alone in the forests or mountains, that creeping anxiety without cause, that mixed feeling of exuberance and awe, is said to be the attendance of Pan by your side: his manic, frenzied presence, that can inspire fear and to which he gave his name: panic.'*

---

*Tacita Dean, from 'A Panegyric', in *Cy Twombly Cycles and Seasons*, ed. Nicholas Serrota, Tate, 2008.

///

For 48 hours, over a weekend when Enrico was away, I was convinced I had tachycardia. I felt my pulse accelerate; I couldn't sleep. I had lunch at my parents' house that Sunday. But on my way home, to reassure myself I stopped by a pharmacy where they took my blood pressure: 124 beats per minute. The pharmacist advised me to ask for a doctor's home visit. Since I was alone that weekend, Thomas comes to wait with me for the doctor to arrive. I don't tell him that I'm sure I'm dying. The doctor does an electrocardiogram in my bedroom. Nothing abnormal there. He suggests prescribing anti-anxiety medication.

///

It is night. We are on the side of the road, with a woman wearing a raincoat, barefoot, who is running. We hear her jagged breath. She is fleeing something. The black and white of the image brings out the white marks in the ground and the blinding searchlight of the lighthouse. She desperately sticks out her hand, trying to get a car to stop. It is only by running into the middle of the road, hands raised, that she manages to get the driver of a convertible to stop. The guy doesn't seem very interested in what might have led a half-naked young woman to be running by the side of the road in the middle of the night. She gets in next to him. We hear her tears and breathing continue over the opening credits of the film (*Kiss Me Deadly*, by Robert Aldrich, 1955), mixing with Nat King Cole's 'Rather Have the Blues,' which is playing on the radio. On the screen, the road, seen from behind the windshield, slides by.

///

'Tacita' means 'silence'. In an interview with Hans Ulrich Obrist, Tacita Dean recounts having written her thesis at the Slade School of Fine Art in London, where she was studying, on Cy Twombly and silence. Later, she tried to make a radio show about silence. She recorded the sound of the silence just before a storm. Although she has never been able to verify this information, she has been told that in nautical terms, the word 'tacita' designates the precise moment before a storm.

///

When air circulates normally, breathing and the breath offer our bodies a kind of verticality that allows us to resolve, respond, decide, participate. To be deprived of these elements is to risk swallowing or inhaling the greenhouse mud. The greenhouse can take many forms – for example books, inheritances, workplaces (we might think, perhaps, of the Bordeaux school as a kind of hothouse) – all those parts of our lives that condition us. It can take a bizarrely long time to realise that we can't breathe correctly in a given place. Sometimes without knowing it, we evolve in spaces and environments which constrict the available air. Scott's fear – of seeing Zelda break the glass ceiling of the greenhouse and escaping – is still just as legitimate.

/ / /

A film by the artist Manon de Boer, *Dissonant* (2010), depicts a dancer, alone, performing some choreography. The opening shot frames her tightly: we only see her face as she listens to three violin sonatas by Eugène Ysaÿe, one after the other. Her eyes close from time to time; she concentrates, recalling sensations, or perhaps memories. We come to understand that she is rehearsing this section, making sure she knows the music. We can read the recognition on her face – she smiles or nods at what she hears – and we notice she is already dancing. The music

71

stops. The frame widens. The dancer sets off, without music. She will perform the same series of movements six times. We no longer hear anything besides her breathing, which paces the choreography. Time is suspended. Her breath guides her: vital, tense; it is the source of her energy. I came across this film in March 2014, when I was asked to write some short texts about the artist for the Printemps de septembre in Toulouse. Manon and I corresponded by email, and I asked her about her film. Its subject isn't only rehearsal, but a form of erosion; the choreography can't be perfectly reproduced six times. 'The nuances that you see are not in the choreography,' Manon told me, 'but were made by mistake or through exhaustion, because the choreography is very physical and difficult.' 'Through exhaustion': breathing, and breath, are tools we can learn to use. Fatigue, however, is a whole other story.

'She smiled vaguely. She might have been thirty or thirty-five. She had dark brown eyes and delicate features. The vague smile barely exposed her teeth, which were small and even. Roucart approached the young woman, continuing to address her as "dear child" and talking in an avuncular tone as his big blue eyes roved up and down her slim form. He declared himself greatly astonished to see her here – first because she never went shooting and secondly because she had said her goodbyes to everyone the previous afternoon and taken a taxi to the station.

"As surprises go, this beats all. And such a pleasant one too," he exclaimed, and she unslung her 16-gauge shotgun, turned it on him, and before he had finished smiling emptied both barrels into his gut.'

Jean-Patrick Manchette, *Fatale*
trans. Donald Nicholson-Smith
New York Review Books Classics, 2011

3. FATIGUE

'Pale and feeble by the side of its original'*

Translated by Ruth Diver

* From Eleanor Marx's introduction to the first edition of her translation of *Madame Bovary*, Great Russell Street, 1886, p. xxi–xxii, cited in: Emily Apter, 'Biography of a translation: *Madame Bovary* between Eleanor Marx and Paul de Man', *Translation Studies*, 2008, 1:1.

When I first met Katinka in September 2014, just after the private view of her show at the Jocelyn Wolff Gallery, we talked about fatigue. I asked her what she thought people really meant when they say that they suffer from fatigue. She explained that in German, the term *müde* describes physical fatigue, the need to sleep at nightfall. We agreed that this did not suit the French word *fatigue*, which describes something else. She said she was surprised, for example, that French parents would sometimes say "*Tu me fatigues*" to their children. This discussion was the beginning of a continuing conversation, and of a great friendship and collaboration that has lasted to this day. It was the starting point for an essay that I am writing about her work, in which I expand on the idea of fatigue in relation to the objects that it creates: 'Part of the humour in Katinka's objects has to do with the fact that they seem to share our predicament. Their weaknesses […] are a reflection of ours. This "fatigue" is not a result of any failure in their fabrication, but rather of the life that these objects live once they are created, and which sometimes leads them to bend, to bow, to slightly collapse.'* Of course, using the word 'fatigue' about these sculptures is a result of our identifying with them: we seem to have something in common with these collapsed, deflated, slumped objects. That projection, that sympathy, is what characterises fatigue: it can leave physical traces – on our faces, in our voices, our muscles – but above all, it is a state that we describe out loud, that we put into words, that we wish to discuss.

///

I'm listening to a lecture on YouTube by the philosopher Judith Butler, titled 'Vulnerability and Resistance'. The words she had written on vulnerability in 'Can One Lead a Good Life in a Bad Life?' had stayed in my memory: '[W] e are, as bodies, vulnerable to others and to institutions, and this vulnerability constitutes one aspect of the social modality through which bodies persist. The issue of my or your vulnerability implicates us in a broader political problem of equality and inequality, since vulnerability can be projected and denied

---

* 'Squirrels to Nuts', in *Katinka Bock*, Les Laboratoires d'Aubervilliers, 2015.

(psychological categories), but also exploited and manipulated (social and economic categories) in the course of producing and naturalizing forms of social inequality.'* The idea that 'bodies persist' despite or rather because of precarity had affected me. I'm trying to explore this idea. Butler's voice is soft, it flows smoothly, it leads me straight into slumber. I fall asleep. In the dream I have, which I remember snatches of, I'm walking in slow motion towards a bus stop. I go past a building that I know well, since it is located just across the boulevard that my apartment windows look out onto. We face each other every day. It's a corner building with no architectural qualities, but I have looked at it so much that I know every single one of its details. On the ground floor, there is a café I often go to: Le Métro. I am obsessed with this building because I am sure that it is entirely unoccupied. My recent insomnia has confirmed this: nobody lives on any of its six floors. I think this is scandalous, but I don't know who to raise this with. In my dream, I try to walk to the bus stop, but my steps are impeded – as if the building was drawing me towards itself, forcing me to slow down.

---

* https://www.radicalphilosophy.com/article/
can-one-lead-a-good-life-in-a-bad-life?

///

'I was tired of being a woman,
tired of the spoons and the pots,
tired of my mouth and my breasts,
tired of the cosmetics and the silks.
There were still men who sat at my table
Circled around the bowl I offered up.
The bowl was filled with purple grapes
And the flies hovered in for the scent
And even my father came with his white bone.
But I was tired of the gender of things.'*

///

I've known ever since I started this research
that I want to talk about fatigued voices. I am
attracted by the word 'fatigued' because I use
it often and wonder what it actually means,
and whether it was used as much in the past.
I imagine fatigue as a garment that you put
on and then take off, or that you wear care-
lessly, or that you cover yourself in completely,
depending on the kind of space you happen to
be in – home, work, a friend's, a lover's. Fatigue
shadows us, overtakes us, disguises us. It can
be identified as a complaint. In speaking about

---

*Anne Sexton, 'Consorting with Angels' (1963).

our fatigue, we are also trying to share something that exists only through the act of saying it. And yet, this state is difficult to describe – it is general, vague, fragile, physical and psychological all at once. I think that if fatigue is shared, then something is produced. I'm searching for what fatigued voices create.

/ / /

In 2013, I was one of the organisers of a seminar that was part of 'Travelling Féministe', a research project created around the Centre Audiovisuel Simone de Beauvoir.* Its aim was to invite researchers or artists to join a critical discussion of the use of images from a feminist and queer perspective. Several sessions were organised, one of them with So Mayer, a poet, writer and teacher who lives in London and who presented *Daughter Rite*, a film directed by Michelle Citron in 1978. The film is organised around two distinct modalities. The first is a montage of home movies made by the filmmaker's father in the

_____

*Founded in 1982 by Delphine Seyrig, Carole Roussopoulos and Ioana Weider, feminist activists who were all involved in film- or video-making, the Centre collects and conserves audio-visual documents about women's history, struggles and rights. Its present director is Nicole Fernandez Ferrer.

1950s. They show two little girls (Michelle and her sister) and their mother, as they are busy with ordinary everyday activities. These images are slightly slowed down and repeated. A voice-over, which can be identified as the voice of one of the two little girls, talks about the relationship she has with her mother. The other part of the film appears at first to be a kind of documentary, which features two young women – two sisters. You see them talking in different rooms of a house (a bedroom, a kitchen). They also talk about their mother, her life, her choices. You understand at the end of the film that these scenes are not improvised, but rather acted, written. The film is built on the following strategy: the home movies – the 'real' documentary images – are reworked and manipulated, whereas the ostensibly improvised scenes, on the other hand, are actually fiction. This twist creates a strong sense of confusion, which has the effect of disorienting the viewer. What interests me, however, is the voiceover in the first part. It is the voice of the filmmaker. Its tone makes the film almost painful to watch: the voice is a drawl, slightly apathetic, almost asleep. It adds to the immodesty that characterises the account of the mother-daughter relationship, placing it in a particularly unflattering context. It begins like this:

'I started this film when I was twenty-eight.
My twenty-eighth birthday was particularly
difficult for me. For months before, I was
depressed, waking up anxious almost
every morning at 5 a.m., having trouble
falling asleep at night, losing weight. I had
trouble working, concentrating, focusing
my attention. Twenty-eight was so old, so
final. Just before my birthday I suddenly
remembered that in my mother's twenty-
eighth year she had married and then
had her first child – me. And here I was
entering into my twenty-eighth year, and I
was not married or having a child. Turning
twenty-eight and not doing like my mother,
I realized I was very scared. And it was this
fear on my twenty-eighth birthday that
started the process which has become this
film. I am now thirty. I dedicate this film
with love, to my mother, a woman who I am
very much like and not like at all.'*

The voice in *Daughter Rite* is numb, just like
the slow-motion pictures. The film's capacity to
induce a depressive state is broken by the lively
tone of the dialogue between the two actors in

---

*Extract from the soundtrack of *Daughter Rite*, dir.
Michelle Citron, 1978.

the second part. In the first part, the numbness of the voice and images demands an effort and stamina from the viewer. Fatigue is something that is rarely shown or felt in cinema. *Daughter Rite* endorses a kind of collapse: monotony, routine, exhaustion in its forms and of its models. Feminism is often associated with manifestos or speeches, and is supposed to offer strength and empowerment, but that is not at all the case in Michelle Citron's film.

/ / /

Emma, Eleanor, Emily. Comparative literature professor Emily Apter's essay on Eleanor Marx's translation of *Madame Bovary* is presented as the 'biography of a translation'. Eleanor Marx, the youngest of Karl's daughters, published her translation of Flaubert's novel in 1886. Both Emma's and Eleanor's romantic failures lead them to suicide. What interests Emily is how Eleanor saw her role as translator. Eleanor defends the notion of a 'conscientious translation', one that is honest and sincere, which aims to 'do its best', in order to 'make the original known'. Emily writes: 'Like the cliché, Marx's translation stands as a plea for unoriginal textuality. De-authored, neutered, de-owned – "suicided" if you will – the translation, like the Flaubertian cliché, is cast as an unusual form of literary expression that, counter to Romantic values and myths of avant-garde originality, flaunts its derivativeness and proudly wears the lead weight of predication on literary antecedent.'* Curiously, this idea of unoriginal textuality is connected with fatigue in Apter's essay. Clichés, plagiarism, translation: these are literary operations that play with the exhaustion of language, its depression and chronic fatigue. In September 2016, I wrote to Emily Apter to find out more: 'In the article you wrote about Eleanor Marx and her translation of *Madame Bovary*, you consider the hypothesis of a "fatigued" translation, on the basis of *Le Neutre* by Roland Barthes, and connecting this idea to the notion of "cliché" and loss in the original. I am totally fascinated by this idea. I wanted to confirm that I had read you correctly, and perhaps to ask whether you have expanded on this idea of a "fatigued text" in other publications, notably as it applies to translation. I hope that you will not find this email too intrusive. Your article, as well as your concept of "melo-biographical translation", have been very important to my own research which is also

---

*Emily Apter, 'Biography of a translation: *Madame Bovary* between Eleanor Marx and Paul de Man'.

about methodological questions. Best wishes.' She replied that she had been very intrigued by the idea of textual fatigue but had not explored that pathway any further. The way that Emily described this translation project particularly resonated to my ear: I have the sense that my own research and its re-transcription in the form of a book belong to me less and less. I circle Emily's text again and again: at the same time clinging to her idea of 'unoriginal textuality', which I feel is what I am practising, but also attracted to the expression 'melo-biographical translation'. I wonder if fatigue is giving my project a weepy 'melodramatic' aspect.

///

On 29 November 2017, I receive an email from the SNCF informing me that I have travelled 111,581 kilometres on their trains in three years. The trips between Bordeaux and Paris make up nearly all of that mind-boggling total. I suddenly feel that this number represents the absurdity of my professional life, that it summarises and condenses it better than any other account. I am completely stunned. The circumference of the Earth measures 40,075 kilometres: I have been around the world almost three times just to go to work.

///

I read some writing by Johanna Hedva on the internet ('an anticapitalist psychonaut sorceress who strives to practice an intersectional-feminist, queer, anti-white-supremacist decolonial politics') who is working on illness and its effects, on the basis of personal experience. Her project is called *Sick Woman Theory*. She defines it in these terms: 'a project trying to redefine "sickness" and its perceived binary opposite "wellness". Our concept of being sick comes from capitalism: A sick body is one that cannot work, cannot participate in society in terms of the capitalist notions of labor, value, and product. To "get better" is to be able to go back to work – but what if that condition is never true? What if working is what is making us sick? In SWT, I start from Judith Butler's new premise that the definition of a body is its vulnerability and reliance on infrastructures of support. In other words, to require care, to be sick, to be vulnerable, is not an aberration, but the norm. To be "well" is the oddity.'*

///

*Joanna Hedva interviewed by Vivian Sming, 5 October 2015, https://www.dailyserving.com

Eleanor Marx is very hard on herself when she talks about her translation of Flaubert: 'Certainly no critic can be more painfully aware than I am of the weaknesses, shortcomings, the failures of my work; but at least the translation is faithful. I have neither suppressed nor added a line, a word. [...] My work, then, I know is faulty. It is pale and feeble by the side of its original.'*

My obsession with this empty building is intensifying. It's a mirror. When I look at it, I see myself. All those dark windows, like holes, with no depth. Random pigeons hanging onto the cornices and freezing in the cold. I've been trying to find a drop of light, a sign of life, for months now. The impression it gives me is neither worrying nor sordid. It's more as if the building were tired. Or actually: it's as if this building had taken on my fatigue, my lack of desire, my laziness, my inertia. I could say to myself: 'It's perfect, I've sent my fatigue over to the other side of the street, I've got rid of it.' But no. Just as in my dream, the building is trying to attract me to it. I can't get away from it.

///

---

*Eleanor Marx in the introduction to the first printing of her translation of *Madame Bovary*, London, Great Russell Street, 1886. Cited by Emily Apter, *op.cit.*

According to Anne Sexton, it was with 'The Double Image', a poem written at the end of the 1950s, that she found her voice as a poet. It describes her relationship with her daughter, her trips to hospital, the passing seasons, her certainty that she wants to be a mother. In a recording of her reading the poem, her voice rings out strong, clear, determined. This way of 'saying' a poem depends on a well-cadenced rhythm, controlled, slightly ponderous. That kind of diction seems dated now, and Anne Sexton's voice sounds sad and tired. This 'weak signal' of her voice nevertheless holds an unexpected power: her fatigue is not related to illness, it's rather that it seems to hold the traces of the mountains it needed to move in order to manage to be heard, to be recognised. It sounds as if the silences, the failures, the difficulties (of which there are many, in Anne Sexton's case) through which writing arises are archived in the thickened heaviness of her voice. Fatigue might therefore be a 'methodological' feature, from which one might be able to extract a trove of accounts, a way of doing things, rather than a physical state to be dealt with or masked: that recording of 'The Double Image' makes a condition public that one would ordinarily rather keep hidden. There are many accounts of Anne Sexton's voice: a smoker's voice, deep, steeped in alcohol. When she read, she would often take off her shoes, and speak with a glass in her hand.

/ / /

I didn't so much read Donna Haraway, as much as listen to her and watch her speak. Her voice, along with her hand gestures and lively facial expressions, give off a great sense of energy. I don't know how to use everything that she says, writes or reports – but I often find something that I don't know how to find elsewhere: a way of considering what we collectively consider negatively (failure, pain, illness) as being part of living, and allowing us not only to be creative in different ways, but also to rid ourselves of any kind of cynicism. I sometimes feel that fatigue leads to judgement, to bitter and disembodied rhetoric. That's why I really need the way Donna Haraway deals with depression, in this interview, for example, in order to avoid detachment, to defend our fragilities and the ways they make us less innocent:

> Donna Haraway: Breakdown offers a space of possibility precisely because things don't work smoothly anymore.
> Thyrza Nichols Goodeve: I think that is one of *the* most important things I learned from you.

DH: I like that!

TNG: It's really true.

DH: And of course it's a painful process.

TNG: Yes, but it's exactly the moment where pain can turn into something productive – not to sound too Pollyannaish. Pain is almost a given at moments, so let's see what we can do with it.

DH: Yes, such considerations are always about coming back into a consciousness of finitude, of mortality, of limitation not as a kind of utopian glorification but a condition of possibility. Of creativity in the most literal sense, as opposed to negation. And I feel this is something I learned from feminism too. That insistence on a kind of non-hostile relationship to the mortal body with its breakdowns.*

The question of fatigue demands that we avoid the idea that 'what doesn't kill us makes us stronger'. The ways in which, according to Donna Haraway, we can come up with new 'conditions of possibility' is an answer to dolorist reaction that is all the more powerful in that

---

*Donna J. Haraway, *How Like a Leaf: an interview with Thyrza Nichols Goodeve*, New York, London, Routledge, 1998.

it arises from a feminist tradition that is capable
of accepting the weakening of the body.

/ / /

The artist Frances Stark published a book in
1999 called *The Architect and the Housewife*.
There is a lot of freedom and humour, and
something slightly desperate in the writing of
this work. I was drawn to it for many reasons,
including the fact that I lived with an architect for a long time. When she was writing
this book, Frances Stark was thirty-two years
old. Her questions or problems are numerous:
how to live as an artist, what kind of space
to work in, how to manage financially, how
to overcome heartbreak, eat well, sleep better.
Amid all these questions, the word 'housewife'
regularly appears in her head, along with a
certain anxiety. Associated with the necessarily masculine figure of the architect, the
indoor woman becomes a generic character
that allows Frances Stark to unravel a whole
series of dilemmas, blocks and failures connected with her status as a woman and an
artist. The book is written as a long, loosely
structured monologue, in which references to
her circle, to other artists and architects, or to
writing appear as part of the fabric of everyday

life. And yet, strangely, the monologue always falls on its feet. It unwinds hesitations like loops that never cease to appear, despite the manifest efforts of the author to extract herself from them. The feeling of fatigue that radiates from the text has to do with these infinite loops – but also, more specifically, with the description Frances Stark gives of her ghastly recurring migraines: 'The day I arrived in Taipei to write that essay I had a serious headache, the sick kind, the kind that no amount of pain relievers will abate. I've had them for – what seems like – ever. I am quite accustomed to excusing myself from whatever room I happen to be in, seeking out a soft place for my head, getting there, and await normalcy. Since headaches involve pain that's seemingly located in the brain, confusion may ensue as to where exactly the unpleasant sensation originates. With mostly invisible symptoms, it is easy to think of pain as more of a mental phenomenon and less of a physical one. And, of course, aches in the heads of women have commonly been associated with making excuses for not wanting to "do it".'*

---

* Frances Stark, *The Architect and the Housewife*, London, Bookworks, 1999.

///

In one of the volumes of her autobiography, the writer Vivian Gornick gives amazing descriptions of her mother's mourning period, which she enters and refuses to ever leave, after the death of her husband. Her grief is described as a garment, a blanket or a cloth that she theatrically drapes around herself and which gradually covers her completely. Her voice also takes on this affliction: 'She spoke minimally, and when she did speak her voice was uniformly tight and miserable, always pulling her listener back to a proper recollection of her "condition". If she answered the phone her voice dropped a full octave when she said hello; she could not trust that the caller would otherwise gauge properly the abiding nature of her pain. For five years she did not go to a movie, a concert, a public meeting. She worked, and she suffered.'*

///

In my last year of teaching in Bordeaux, Alexia asked me to supervise her dissertation. She was

---

*Vivian Gornick, *Fierce Attachments*, London, Daunt Books, 2015 (first published by Farrar Strauss and Giroux, New York, 1987).

taking a lot of time deciding what she wanted to write about. During a discussion that we had on the subject in Athens – Alexia is part of a group of students spending six months there – I suggested she start with her wardrobe: Alexia takes great care in the way she dresses. Part of her artistic practice is to create her own clothes. She is always bathed in colour (and has been since childhood), from her hair to her shoes, sequins, pink, gold, with matching lipstick, never red: she engages in new ways of using her clothes every day, with new combinations that she says have something to say about her frame of mind, her desires, her emotions, her laziness. She decided that her dissertation will examine her outfits and the way she sees each day as offering her a new suit of armour. We talk about this a lot. I tell her to read Judith Butler's discussion of our daily costume, the clothing of heteronormative, with all its weight and constraints. We talk about the proliferation effect that her extravagant clothes incarnates, with which she can destabilise established norms, notably those that regulate the functioning of the school in Bordeaux, according to Alexia. In parallel, as we deconstruct her wardrobe together on the basis of the photos that she takes of her outfits day after day, she talks to me about 'The Little Mermaid', the tale by Hans Christian Andersen, that she has chosen to incorporate into her dissertation, and which she is using a copy of as a bookmark. I dive back into the story of the little mermaid who accepts having her voice and her tongue cut out in exchange for a human appearance that will perhaps allow her to find love. One evening in Athens, when we are all seated at a restaurant table and it's starting to get chilly, I ask Alexia, who is going back to her place, to get me a jumper. I never gave it back. It's a huge black woollen cardigan. I wore it all through my pregnancy. By taking it from her wardrobe, which we talked about so much, she created a shelter for me that I kept far beyond Bordeaux and Athens.

/ / /

I met Maïder in Rome, at the Villa Medici. Her face appeared between the shelves in the library. The friendship we share is connected to books – those we exchange, those we talk about, that have been at the heart of our conversations for the last almost ten years. Among the voices surrounding me, and surrounding my research, Maïder's voice, often on the telephone, or like me, in railway stations or on escalators between two trains, is an important one. In February 2015, Maïder and her friend Annie MacDonell, with

whom she makes up a duo of artists for some of
her projects, are giving a reading at the Pompidou Centre. It's a piece written in two voices. As
they read, the pages cover a lit-up table which
projects an image that starts off being grey, then
gradually gets darker. The piece is an account
of their common experience as young artists in
residence at Le Fresnoy – a filmmaking school
in the north of France that takes in students
after their diplomas. They didn't know each
other at the time, and met while they were both
looking for an apartment in Roubaix, where
they were going to have to spend a year. Their
performance piece tells the story of that long
stay in Roubaix, their shared solitude in that
cold apartment, their relationship to the school
and to what they are supposed to be doing
there, the grey skies, how they gradually lost
their bearings. The figure of a horse abandoned
in a field that they pass on their way to the
school appears regularly throughout the text,
a friendly figure, mostly, but one whose lead
rope and loneliness reflected their own sense of
being trapped and powerless. The young women
become attached to the horse, keep an eye out
for it, are glad to see it. As their anxiety grows,
it becomes the only incarnation of what might
save them from their daily environment. Their
sense of depression increases. They both try,

each in different ways, to flee Roubaix but also
to manage to accomplish something there. The
piece they wrote together many years later has
a cyclical structure, whose centre is dominated
by the horse with its lead rope, which appears
again and again like a chorus, a rhyme, that
pushes the story forward but also pulls it back,
and keeps it bogged down with that image. A
disproportionate focus, like something one
might cling to on the edge of a cliff: 'The horse
appeared like an unexpected gift in the middle
of that autumn, which felt like the end of winter,
so long were the days, the dizzying monotony
punctuated by the endless trips to and from
school, the same conversations with the other
students, the same words repeated again and
again till they seemed worn out, the same evenings spent listening on repeat to the same
CDs that Annie's boyfriend had sent her from
Toronto, the same trips to Ghent, Brussels,
Courtrai, attempts at escape which generated
nothing but an inevitable feeling of failure, and,
worst of all, the same killer Sundays, which
left us washed up, each in our own bed, like
two moribund whales. The days seemed to be
melting together into one endless, terrifying day
that time could no longer measure. And so the
discovery of the horse was like a new horizon, or
rather, our only horizon. It became the center of

all my conversations with Annie. We were going to take a series of photos, shoot a film, no, write a more complex script in connection with my recent performance in Paris... Undoubtably, there was power in the poetry of that horse, and we secretly wondered if we were the only ones in that desolate town to grasp it.'* During the reading their voices are flat, lifeless. Their performance perfectly matches the pallidity of their common experience, so much so that for the audience listening to them read, it becomes amusing, dark, then chilling and exhausting as well.

///

'When the sister of illustrious William and Henry James came to the end of her invalid life of confinement, she (Alice James) dropped the tone of humour and spirit so valued by her family and dictated the final entry on her Diary to her nurse and companion, Katherine Loring: 'All through Saturday, the 5th, and even in the night, Alice was making sentences. One of the last things she said to me was to make a

---

* Maïder Fortuné and Annie MacDonell, *Stories are Meaning Making Machines*, unpublished script of the performance.

correction in the sentence of March 4th "moral discords and nervous horrors." This dictation of March 4th was rushing about in her brain all day, and although she was very weak and it tired her much to dictate, she could not get her head quiet until she had it written; then she was relieved...'*

///

I left Bordeaux with presents: Nora gave me a tiny tarot card that I always carry in my wallet for good luck. Hugo gave me a pocketknife, which was made in the school workshops and which I keep, unfolded, on one of my bookshelves. I set it there in such a way that it looks towards that empty building. That gift is watching over me, reminding me to stay vigilant.

---

* From a note in *The Diary of Alice James*, ed. Leon Edel, New York, Dodd, Mead & Co, 1964, cited by Sandra M. Gilbert and Susan Gubar, *The Madwoman in the Attic, The Woman Writer and the Nineteenth-Century Literary Imagination*, Yale University Press, 1979.

The most important thing I have to say today is that hair matters. This is a life lesson my family did not teach me. Wellesley and Yale failed to instill in me: the importance of your hair. Your hair will send very important messages to those around you. It will tell people who you are and what you stand for. What hopes and dreams you have for the world... and especially what hopes and dreams you have for your hair. Likewise your shoes. But really, more your hair. So, to sum up. Pay attention to your hair. Because everyone else will.

Hilary Clinton
Commencement speech
at Yale University, 2001

4. OVERFLOWING

Sentimental being

Translated by Jessica Spivey

The opening scenes of Woody Allen's *Another Woman* (1988), follow Gena Rowlands in a New York apartment which serves as her office. Her character, Marion Post, is a philosopher. She needs quiet to work. At dusk, asleep at her type-writer, she is woken by a voice coming through an air duct that links her apartment to that of a psychoanalyst who lives opposite. She realises that she is directly linked to the consulting room and its visiting patients. Despite the cushions she uses to try and block the wall, the voices invade her space. One most of all: that of Mia Farrow. The content of her sessions breaks into Gena Rowlands' refuge. Intrigued by what she hears, she becomes magnetically drawn to this stranger. The film progressively plays out the consequences of this meeting of two polarised female characters. Marion's clinical reserve, the distance that she thinks she can keep from the world around her, and her characteristic absence of emotion will gradually crumble away on contact with the fears and anxieties of Mia Farrow. Through this sequence I am able to focus in on one thing: the way that voices can break through walls, undoing the partitions between inside and out. Leaking, escaping, roaming, invading. This voice which breaks into this character's existence is the crack from which Marion Post's life slowly begins to fall apart.

///

Many works discuss how women's voices are difficult to hem in, to hold down. I go in search of situations in which women's voices escape and spread. I pause on those which are seen as too lyrical, hallucinatory sometimes, founded on grievance or demands – as though their emotion, sitting too comfortably, makes them socially unacceptable. For these voices, the judgements are often harsh, cutting. They are ignored. But they interest me for exactly this supposed excess. They are liquid, aquatic, acerbic.

///

In the wake of a piece I wrote on her exhibition at *Les Laboratoires d'Aubervilliers*, Katinka and I put our heads together for a public reading, programmed for December 2015. The starting point will be my piece, which I will deliver like a story, based around a series of projected images. One day in mid-August, when we are each on holiday in Italy, corresponding by email and sharing photos, she suggests: 'A table and a chair or two. A glass or two on the table. I divert the tap in the Lab kitchen through a transparent tube. You read your piece. The tap is turned on: some water flows out and fills up the glass. The water spills onto the table and the floor. When your reading is over, I stop the tap. This should be before we find ourselves in an aquarium. I'm thinking of the nasoni drinking fountains in Rome. What do you think?' Our discussions have often led us to plumbing, and piping – which Katinka gets mixed up in wherever she goes. But we also speak of crying, of swimming, of splashing. 'Tears and loving and ideas.' 'We're overflowing!'

It seems logical that water should follow us into the *Laboratoires* studio. The idea then is to let the glass fill up throughout my talk, spreading slowly across the floor, so the audience has to lift up their feet to stop them getting wet. At the very end of my presentation, against the projection of successive images of flooding (from cinema and documentary), Katinka stands up and reads a few lines of 'Water Pipe', a poem by Gertrude Stein:

There is a fire next door.
Did she make it.
Of course some things are lost.
Water trickles.
And pansies. No fennel.
Water-pipes and pencils.
A little water-pipe. I have it here.
Of course you mean a water-pipe.
We watched and saw how they fixed it.
This was a very strange matter.
A little visiting and so speedily done.
Indeed water-pipe.
We said water was not lost.
It isn't.
Not nearly so much wind.
In conclusion I ask for water.
Are you not content with the rain.
I am very content with it.*

There are two musical excerpts included in our presentation: the first goes with the part when the postcards we exchanged over the summer are projected. Parading across the screen are Sicilian landscapes, building sites, a pair of flip-flops abandoned on a beach, sheets of poetry, an outdoor cinema. All the while you hear

---

* Gertrude Stein, 'Water Pipe' (1916), in https://www. persee.fr/

Adriano Celentano's '24 Mila Baci' in tribute to
Italian summers of love. The other song starts
when Katinka has finished reading the extract
from Gertrude Stein, and signals for us to start
folding up our chairs, and those of the audience. We chose Patti Smith's 'Dancing Barefoot',
as we thought this was the time for taking off
our shoes and dancing in the water.

///

Rather than talking about good, upstanding
voices, overflow allows me to collect the more
unruly kinds. I understand that what I call sentimentality is in relationship with disobedience
or with the liberties that we take. Through my
discussions with Katinka, I also understand that
it is the details and everyday actions – caught in
the motion of our projects and desires – that
guide us towards these margins, and not the
other way round. Adriano Celentano, poetry,
love, Rome and tears – all these were necessary
to make the speaker's cup spill over.

///

The off-feminine voices which interested me
at the start of my research (those of 1940's
Hollywood) bear stories woven from emotion.

The stories they tell are not so much intended to move a narrative forward as to document the affects that course through the protagonists. Tonalities, murmurs, whispers, breath: so much detail that is harder to spot, or to hear in the smoother, more consistent, voices of men. These affects make the voices more vulnerable, more lyrical, more empathetic. Take the opening sequence of Hitchcock's *Rebecca* (1940): with its confused dreamer's tale of an opening title. It is Joan Fontaine speaking. Her voice is entwined with the undulating camera footage; somewhat hallucinatory, particularly agile and sensitive as it breaks through the gates at Manderley, plunged in fog. The voice quivers, it recalls. While later on the film shows Joan Fontaine (the lead character) as the object of rejection – sent back to her incompetence, her inability to play the adroit lady of the house – these first minutes are filled with a nervous enthusiasm, recalled somewhat feverishly – clearly attributed to this nameless character, this unequivocal source of the utterance, who is 'replacing' Rebecca. Tied to phantom bodies, the voices recounting their dreams, or more simply their lives, in classical cinema fall out of sync with the bodies on-screen. The voice-off, unlike any other technological process, allows a departure from the

synchronised system. While house arrest rules
this school of cinema, in the moment of separation, female characters attain a new status.
Given the luxury of seeing the story unfold,
like any other spectator, with their voices float-
ing above the image, these characters gain a
privileged point of view, which had rarely been
reserved for them. This is the opening dream of
Rebecca, but also the story told by Joan Craw-
ford in *Mildred Pierce* (1945), and the voice of
Barbara Stanwyck in *All I Desire* (1953).

///

If these are voices trying to escape, it's because
their spaces (or stories) are shutting them in
– and sometimes these are spaces they have
themselves created. Twenty years after publication, Angela Carter writes a postface for her
novel *Love*, the tale of an unlikely love triangle
between an unstable young woman and two
batshit crazy brothers in provincial England. It's
a very dark book. In the postface, Angela Carter
decides to draw out the initial story. Then I
thought that perhaps the best way of discussing the novel would really be to write a bit more
of it […] the people in *Love* would now be edging
up to the middle age they thought could never
happen, they thought that the world would end

first.'* She returns to each character, envisaging what he or she becomes, in light of the political and social developments that had taken place since 1969. The postface is much more inventive than the novel, which struck me as very serious. The narrative solutions, sketched out in a few lines twenty years on, are more sarcastic and above all more feminist, their tone radically different from the original. Faster, funnier and much more present, Angela Carter's voice spills the destinies of her heroes, imagining new ramifications for them, or on the contrary, drowning them with gusto.

///

Curiously, tales of drowning, and stories of fluid and flux, come along with overflowing voices. 'Bathroom Contemplation' is a text written by Haegue Yang in 2000, as part of a series dedicated to Gertrude Stein. The artist is now 29 and has left Korea, and a very politically active family in which she always felt like the black sheep, for Germany. We discuss this text together on Skype in March 2017. I am curious about the way she writes. Her explanations

---

* Angela Carter, 1987 postface to *Love*, Vintage (1971), 2006.

help me understand how she sees literature. She describes her career to me as sown with traps; personal and professional, linked to her exile and the different languages that inhabit her, and also linked to writing which she sees as a difficult, uncomfortable practice, like an emergency tool that has a particular faculty for capturing vulnerability. 'Bathroom Contemplation' has since acquired the status of a work in its own right. At a Haegue retrospective, organised at the Ludwig Museum in Cologne in 2018, I saw it exhibited, in A4 format, hung up on the wall. Through its construction, the writing creates a temporal grey area. At the heart of its anecdotes is a domestic incident that took place when the artist's mother came to stay: the overflowing of the bathtub after she had taken a bath. This maternal visit in many respects seems fruitless, a failure. The mother and daughter's routines for communal life have worn thin and don't patch together well. After this experience, the artist suggests to her mother, who is a writer, that they write down and then exchange their versions of this story, as a way of repairing the damage. 'Bathroom Contemplation' is the result of this exchange. It is cut into fifteen short paragraphs, numbered quite randomly and written as a duet. It piles up a series of negative emotions: shame,

embarrassment, awkwardness, resentment, dis-
satisfaction, shyness.

'One day my mom took a bath. I was working
on my computer in the living room. After
vaguely hearing that my mom was done, I also
heard her start mumbling or complaining a bit.
I kept working. It had been just too much over
the last several weeks, so I felt I had a right to
ignore her, just once. She was asking me why
the water was not draining away. I really, desperately, did not want to be disturbed in that
moment. [...] I walked into the bathroom and
found it full of water! [...] I started harshly to
give her the blame, and said we needed to dry
up quickly in order not to disturb the neigh-
bour living below us. Finally, I released all my
stress and anger at once. It took me a while to
slowly calm down. Once I had relaxed a bit, I felt
sorry for her. I felt so sad for both of us. [...] My
mother seemed much smaller to me than she
ever was. It hurt me very much.'*

The work takes the path of rehabilitation.
Filled with good intentions, highly energetic and
tenacious, it feels like there is a power within it:
liberating the author from these feelings of awkwardness and failure. The act of complaining, of

---

*Haegue Yang, 'Bathroom Contemplation', in *How to
Write* no 4, Berlin, Wiens Verlag, 2001.

blaming and reproaching each other for things is put through the precise sieve of literature and becomes the circumstances of life and of work. In the most literal sense, this piece of writing about a piping system is the best possible way to evacuate emotions that on the face of things seem troublesome. The episode of the overflowing bathtub is treated in a tragi-comic manner by mother and daughter. But the analogy of tension remains (not only between the two women, but also between the German and Korean cultures, which distance them) of a word that won't come out or is taken the wrong way, of a relaxation that fails to set in. The bath and the water are like fleeting, flowing metaphors of a vital system that is supposed to bring well-being and relaxation. The work fundamentally raises a question of comfort: the thing that allows us to feel ourselves in a place we don't know, which might (or might not) be felt with family and which we don't always manage to find in our work.

/ / /

Interiors, rooms, bathrooms, the houses that confine, that shut in and that show up feminine incompetence even though they (the women) are supposed to know what to do there, supposed to have the knack for it.

Domestic space, as in the story of Haegue Yang and the overflowing bath, is supposed to offer a certain comfort – a security of the kind that is often sought and rarely found. It's the same story for the character of Gena Rowlands or that of Joan Fontaine: will these women manage to feel at home in their houses, or should they treat these with caution, with trepidation? The overflowing voices give an echoing response to our own overflow of domestic discomforts or failures: each expressing the difficulty of finding the conditions for a good life.

/ / /

In *The Acoustic Mirror*, which mainly deals with Hollywood cinema in the 1940s, the art historian and theorist Kaja Silverman writes: 'The female subject's gaze is depicted as partial, flawed, unreliable and self-entrapping. She sees things that aren't there, bumps into walls or loses control at the sight of the color red. And although her own look seldom hits its mark, woman is always on display before the male gaze [...] Woman's words are shown to be even less her own than her "looks." They are scripted for her, extracted by an external agency, or uttered by her in a trance-like state. Her voice reveals a remarkable facility for self-disparagement and self-incrimination – for putting the blame on Mame. Even when she speaks without apparent coercion, she is always spoken from the place of the sexual other.'

///

Jane Eyre is a metrological novel, with windswept moors filled with currents of air and the cold; with ghosts and unlikely diseases, and huge houses lost in a hostile landscape. Soon after her arrival at Thornfield Hall where she is hired as a governess, Jane Eyre is woken from her sleep by a woman's voice in the night: 'I hardly know whether I had slept or not after this musing; at any rate, I started wide awake on hearing a vague murmur, peculiar and lugubrious, which sounded, I thought, just above me. I wished I had kept my candle burning: the night was drearily dark; my spirits were depressed. I rose and sat up in bed, listening. The sound was hushed. I tried again to sleep; but my heart beat anxiously: my inward tranquillity was broken.' She hears the sound of footsteps. Fear sets in. She is slowly falling asleep again, when a demonic laugh rings out, a 'goblin-laugher' and 'unnatural sound'. 'Something gurgled and moaned. Ere long, steps retreated up the gallery towards the third-storey staircase: a

door had lately been made to shut in that staircase; I heard it open and close, and all was
still.'* The mad woman locked up in the attic is
Bertha Mason, the first wife of Edward Roches-
ter – the master of Thornfield Hall and guardian
of the little girl in Jane's charge. He met her
in Jamaica, just after he finished his studies,
and was seduced by her beauty. He marries
her quickly, too quickly, without getting to
know her. He later learns that Bertha's mother
was mad, and that a long line of madness and
mental illness runs through her family history.
He brings his wife back to England and for ten
years keeps her locked up in the attic. He keeps
trying to forget this first part of his life. But he
falls in love with Jane and this woman's voice
escapes from the borders of the house and tips
the novel on its side. Yet Bertha's story is never
told by Bertha. She is never given speech.

/ / /

'Woman never speaks the same way,' writes the
feminist philosopher Luce Irigaray. 'What she
emits is fluent, fluctuating, and she is not listened to unless the proper meaning (meaning

---

*Charlotte Bronte, *Jane Eyre*, Wordsworth Classics,
1999.

of the proper) is lost. Whence the resistances to
that voice which overflows the "subject". Which
the subject then congeals, freezes, in its categories until it paralyses the voice in its flow.'*

///

In November 2014 I was invited by François and
Thomas to take part in a symposium on mood in
Lyon. The event, called 'Moody', looked to trace
the relation between emotions, the soul and our
modern age. Their proposal said the following:
'Distinct from *feeling*, as the external projection
of interiority, *mood* is the transformation of a
receptive individual to their environment, the
product of sensitive attention to the world.' For
the first time I collected all the questions and
characters that women's voices were whispering to me. My contribution was called 'Ladies'
Voices', after a work by Gertrude Stein, written
in 1916, which I had then just come across. The
piece was three pages long. It was a short play
in four acts, with a curtain rise, and it illus-
trates Stein's interest in the spoken word – she
devised the play from real discussions that she

---

*Luce Irigaray, *This Sex Which Is Not One*, trans.
Catherine Porter and Carolyn Burke, Cornell
University Press, 1985.

had overheard – as well as in the art of convers-
ing with empty space. She was inspired to write
the play by a stay in Majorca, in a hotel fre-
quented by expatriates from all walks of life. A
place where different languages would mix; with
attempts at speech interrupted, always aborted,
to advance, or simply to keep afloat the game
of society, with its stock replies and attempts
at courtesy. Gossip, as a social and discursive principal, allows the undoing of notion of
authorship. It belongs to everyone and no one.
'What are ladies' voices.' The sentence, thrown
into the middle of the text, without a question
mark, opens possibilities. Women's voices carry
the domestic kingdom with not-always-veiled
criticisms, social hypocrisies, weather forecasts
and denied ambitions. All this surfaces in the
play. Gossip is without limits, it brims over the
body (both that of speaker and listener), it floats
in the air and evades the 'high' forms of writing
and conversation alike. Its trivial power makes
it a fleeing subject that dominant culture will
always consider as digression. Gossip can also
be a tone, a note, a tale, a fable or a theatre
sketch. I hold onto its melodic texture.

/ / /

Writing about how she became immersed in

the witchcraft of Bocage, Jeanne Favret-Saada explains the extent to which, as an ethnographer, she found it impossible to observe this phenomenon from the outside. She has to take part in, and herself become a subject of, her intended study. She finds herself undergoing a series of reactions that slip out of her control, transfixing her with their intensity. She only has her field journal as an archive of her meetings with the enchanted and the 'dewitchers': a record which she does not use straight away. 'I organised my field journal so that I might make something of it later on. My notes were maniacally precise, so that one day I might rehallucinate the experience and so (because I would no longer be "caught" in it but rather "recaptured") finally understand them.'* The journal in question follows a precise template: no private or subjective opinions, only a gathering of information. The overspilling of experience produces a temporal disjunction: 'In the instant one is most affected, one cannot recount the experience. In the moment it is recounted, one cannot understand it.' I make note of the idea that we could train this 'rehallucination'.† That

---

*Jeanne Favret-Saada, *The Anti-Witch*, trans. Matthew Carey, HAU Books, 2015.
† Ibidem.

it could be postponed – and most importantly that this could be seen as necessary for work – opens avenues.

/ / /

The main character in Nanni Moretti's *Mia Madre* (2015) seems completely lost, forsaken: her mother is dying, she has reached a block with the film she is supposed to be directing. One night she has a nightmare. She wakes with a jolt. She sits up in bed. Bringing her feet to the floor, she realises it is covered in water. She turns on the light and finds that there has been a water leak while she was sleeping. The passage through the dream and its violence, the night, the cold, the water all across the floor: its sense of unease is complete and chilling. The idea that a water leak might occur in the middle of the night seems worse than a nightmare to me. The scene makes an impression on me because I associate it with those fleeing voices, hallucinatory and challenging domestic comfort, that *home sweet home* turned anxiogenic.

/ / /

Sara Ahmed's book, *Living a Feminist Life*, is presented as a manual. I pause on the passages that talk about complaining. They borrow in part from her blog, 'feministkilljoys'. The book and the blog were written as mirror images, at the same time. She introduces herself like this: 'My name is Sara Ahmed and this is my research blog. I am a feminist killjoy. It is what I do. It is how I think. It is my philosophy and my politics.'

At the start of her blog she announces that complaint – as a mode of expression, a mode of speech, a way of being – will be at the heart of her next book. The accounts she gathers focus on the effects of women's complaints in institutional and academic contexts, the risks that are run; the intimate way that complaints are built before they find a public form; the temporal specificity of complaint; the judgements which it exposes one to. She writes of the paradoxes she observes: 'the reasons making a complaint is difficult are the same reasons that making a complaint is necessary.'*

The word 'institution' can hold a lot: the couple, the family, work. Women are said to complain a lot. I also complain a lot. But I find people who don't complain weird. I used to complain a lot about the art school where

---

*Sara Ahmed, https://feministkilljoys.com/2017/
11/03/cutting-yourself-off

I taught; I complained about the way that the leadership used its authority; the way that we teachers made space for it, despite ourselves; about the lack of horizontality. I complained about the students, and how they acted like visitors in their own school; I found that the very idea of pedagogy was losing its meaning. I never confused these moments of complaint with a falling out of love, or disillusion. These criticisms spoke rather to the extent to which cracks and imperfections are the starting point that make work possible. Complaint is also a form of realignment, a very necessary form of critical revival. I am not surprised when I read that for Sara Ahmed, complaining is a form of feminist pedagogy.

/ / /

Henry James' novels featured in my teenage reading. I remember a trip to Italy with Eva and Lila where, with all three of us slumped on our rucksacks waiting for some youth hostel to open, I would read them passages from *The Golden Bowl*. I now realise just how generous they were – it isn't a book that lends itself to reading aloud. Henry James builds up looping effects: people say things to each other without really saying them, grey areas are upheld with all the power of a lie; silence and its secrets reign, even at the heart of conversation and attempts at explanation. All that remains are obsessions, outpourings which once put into words seem like architectural lunacies: projections which have lost any contact with reality, where the extent of their abstraction almost raises a smile, verging on absurdity. But these outpourings are necessary, they always end up serving a stylistic purpose. They allow for the void to be evacuated and put in order. In her work on performativity, the feminist theorist Eva K. Sedgwick quotes a passage from *The Golden Bowl*: "'I don't care what you make of it, and I don't ask anything whatever of you – anything but this. I want to have said it – that's all; I want not to have failed to say it. To see you once and be with you, to be as we are now and as we used to be, for one small hour – or say for two – that's what I have had for weeks in my mind. I mean, of course, to get it BEFORE – before what you're going to do [...] This is what I've got. This is what I shall always have. This is what I should have missed, of course," she pursued, "if you had chosen to make me miss it [...] I had to take the risk. Well, you're all I could have hoped. That's what I was to have said. I didn't want simply to get my time with you, but I wanted you to know. I wanted you" – she kept it up, slowly, softly, with a small tremor of voice, but without the least failure of sense or sequence – "I wanted you to understand. I wanted you, that is, to hear. I don't care, I think, whether you understand or not. If I ask nothing of you I don't – I mayn't – ask even so much as that. What you may think of me – that doesn't in the least matter. What I want is that it shall always be with you – so that you'll never be able quite to get rid of it – that I DID. I won't say that you did – you may make as little of that as you like. But that I was here with you where we are and as we are – I'm just saying this [...] That's all."*

Sedgwick is struck by the circularity of the monologue. What is this woman talking about? It is impossible to say for sure: an unrequited love, a long overdue exchange – following many attempts. This fragment is an overflow, a discharge, a leak. The voice, its plaintive meanders, its insistence on the 'I', which punctures the passage like a flag, or a staple – a rigid and demanding tool; and yet the language is aquatic, swamp-like, it submerges, it is borderless.

///

---

* Henry James, *The Golden Bowl*, 1904.

I listen to interviews with the historian Arlette Farge, where she speaks about her work and her research. She talks about how she has allowed emotion to guide her editing, and the way she brings ideas together. She allows this emotion to gather in speed, becoming less a subject, or theme of her work, than a method. Overflow becomes a way of working: 'In *La Vie Fragile*, there are a few pages about emotion; for me there is nothing sloppy about emotion – I think I say as much in the book – but a kind of opening, a bursting of intelligence, a breach. When the book came out in 1986, there weren't many of us female historians in France. Leaning into your feelings and saying that you were working from emotion – that was perilous as it meant working from a feminine perspective. All the same, I undertook some linguistic research into what the word *émotion* contains: its links with words like "move", "motive" and "mutiny". You can see, in short, that emotion is not the receptacle of all the world's tears, but on the contrary is something active.' This is what I am looking for in my overflowing: a way of under-standing feelings that doesn't rule out acuity or activism. Outpourings can find a place in a shared space, that of work, of the city, of an interaction, turning away from the confines of the home. I acutely feel how narrow is the ledge,

how the voices I am collecting are on a verge
and risk tumbling off into madness.

///

'For it is not the woman who first calls her self-
articulation a complaint, a whine, a plea,' writes
theorist Lauren Berlant, a specialist in emotions
and their political implications. 'Rather, the
patriarchal social context in which she makes
her utterance hystericizes her, even before she
speaks. As a euphemism for menstruation, "the
female complaint" typifies the banality of female
suffering: every month we (that is, those who
can think of the woman as Other) hear woman's
litany of the ills done to her, but we can't be
moved by it, because she brought it on herself,
she's weak, that's just the way she is. The female
complaint is thus an aesthetic "witnessing" of
injury. Situated precisely in the space between
a sexual politics that threatens structures of
patriarchal authority and a sentimentality
that confirms the inevitability of the speaker's
powerlessness, the female complaint registers
the speaker's frustration, rage, abjection, and
heroic self-sacrifice, in an oppositional utterance that declares its limits in its very saying.'*

---

*Lauren Berlant, 'The Female Complaint'.

/ / /

Kaja Silverman's book, which I previously cited, like Mary Ann Doane's *The Desire to Desire*, is one of the works that came out in the 1980s and marked out a feminist examination of cinema which we still depend on. Researchers, critics and professors at various American universities now work from the radical re-reading of Hollywood Cinema, as she dismantled it. The scope of their critical expression, precision of their analysis and their freedom of tone stick to a model – notably because as a feminist field, cinema is up there with literature, psychoanalysis and critical theory. One of the chapters in *The Desire to Desire*, delves into the idea of female spectatorship, in what Hollywood does with what she calls 'medical discourse' films – *The Cat People* (1942), *Possessed* (1947), *The Locket* (1946), *Beyond the Forest* (1949) – in which female characters are subjected to a particularly invasive clinical masculine gaze. Culturally, female spectators are attributed with an excess of emotion, feelings, affect and empathy. The 'women's films' in the 1940s were often classed as *weepies* – films which would hit an emotional vein. They were also often films featuring sick women. Mary Ann Doane goes on to analyse the word 'sympathy': both in physiology

129

and medicine, sympathy denotes a form of contagion between different bodies – too great an affinity. In the cinema, the female gaze would engage closely with an image in a limitless identification. The lack of a need to establish any distance is taken care of in these films, in the same way as you would treat a 'pathology'.

///

In these examples from film, women are isolated because they are seen as unwell. A male gaze and discourse arranges this isolation. To me, it seems that the female voices, when they overflow, stimulate the sympathy evoked by Mary Ann Doane, but in a different way: the movement that sends them off the handle is above all a way of making contact with other voices. Their active surface suddenly grows; touching and brushing against other bodies or lives. In these moments, the voice is no longer an object to be studied, but a basis for acquaintance, a meeting point. Once shared, sentimentality becomes a force to connect, to bring together – the women spectators as well as the actors, and so the line separating these two poles starts to blur. Contagion feels good.

'It gets harder as you get older, as your positions become entrenched and your relationships become entrenched. It's not so easy to flit around. But I guess just for me personally when I look at my life, you know, I have a pretty staid life, I'm married, I teach, I'm no kind of Bukowski or Hemingway running around the world having wild experiences, so it kind of – the place where I try and be free is in my reading, it would kill me if not only this part of my life is so staid but also my reading I shut down, you know, then there would be no hope, and I think also for a writer who has come out of books – and many writers don't. Some writers come from experience, some writers come from trauma, there are all different kinds of writers, but I obviously am a writer who came out of other books, so my whole arena, the way I can move forward is through reading creatively.'

Zadie Smith
From the transcript of an interview with Paul Holdengräber recorded at the New York Public Library 22 Nov. 2010

5. SPEED

I'm the Taxi Woman

Translated by Clem Clement

April 16, 2018: my sister Lola, who has just started a new job as Advocacy Officer for Refugees/Migrants at Amnesty International, is on the radio, on Europe 1 – the midday Europe debate. For the first time, live. Time is of the essence. It's a tense week; the National Assembly is about to vote on the Asylum and Immigration Bill. She has to talk about the increase in length of immigrant detention periods. Reducing processing times for asylum claims could be a good thing, she says: the faster people can gain asylum, the better their outcomes. The problem is that, as things stand, shortening processing times infringes on human rights. Refugees face more obstacles than ever in accessing rights and in having their voices heard during the asylum application period. The interviewer counters: 'Asylum seekers have more rights than ever. The ideal outcome of an asylum claim is to have an answer as soon as possible, and the French government's response times are very long, leaving immigrants in difficult situations because they can't work for the first few months. The new law is trying to correct this. Do you agree, Lola Schulmann?' 'No, absolutely not. That kind of argument usually tries to differentiate between good and bad asylum seekers. These are people who have experienced a traumatic migration process and a lot of violence. Understanding the French system and how it works, finding a lawyer, gathering documents, putting together an appeal, it all takes time. So, changing the appeal window from thirty to fifteen days is extremely worrying,' she replies. I listen to the live recording two hours after the broadcast. I don't recognise her voice. I hear its tension, the way the words jostle in her mouth, some swallowed up by speed and the need to make sense straight away, to be efficient. I'm not used to hearing such a familiar voice on the radio, and so I'm outraged when they cut her off mid-sentence. Jonathan, a friend of Enrico's, will say after hearing it that Lola's voice is a mixture of my other sister Fanny's and my own.

///

The voice is a tool, a technique, often put under strain: time is of the essence. I am concerned about the effects of speed on the voice and therefore on the meaning of what is said. On the one hand, speed obstructs breathing, creates tension and distorts meaning. But moments of rapidity fascinate me. In the cinema, I pay attention to the rhythms of dialogue, listening for accelerations that mark dizzying shows of virtuosity.

///

I love *The West Wing*. Seven seasons, all faithful to the long-take and 'walk-and-talk' format in which words and discussions, ever more expert and complex, follow an unrelenting rhythm. The endless corridors of the White House are filled with a high-speed traffic of bodies and ideas. Since no social interaction is free from the urgency of the decisions to be made, every relationship – and every conversation – takes on a keen intensity. The most brilliant among the crowd of assistants, advisors, presidents and secretaries is a female character, C.J. Cregg. As press secretary for the White House, she is the key character who finds, shapes and invents the words, the vocabulary and the turns of phrase that will intensify or rewrite the President's message. C.J. Cregg is breathtaking: her diction, the sound of her voice, her sense of humour, her laughter, how the series weighs

137

her down with ever more responsibility and
how she deals with it. In Season 1, there is an
evening party in the White House, the shadowed
offices humming with a muted and secretive
atmosphere of celebration. Champagne glasses
in hand, the staff gather around C.J. as she
lip-syncs the hip-hop song 'The Jackal'. What
could be more appropriate for a spokesper-
son than performing lyrics she hasn't written
herself? 'The Jackal' is a rap song written by
Ronny Jordan in 1993 for his album *The Quiet
Revolution*. It tells the story of a man nicknamed
the Jackal, king of the streets in the 1970s, a
'lady's man', a crook in rhinestones and Italian
suits. The song is written from a woman's perspective, and was performed by the poet Dana
Bryant, a star of the 1990s spoken-word scene
in New York, who was known for her glamorous
appearances in a gold lamé dress. Grace Jones,
but more ferocious. She says: 'Yeah, when I'm
just doing readings, or choreo-poems, like acted
monologues, I just wear jeans, but to reach a
club crowd you definitely need extra things. The
guys are sitting there in the front row thinking
"Aw no, she ain't gonna do that poetry shit", so
that's what the gold dress is for. You have to
come on like a chanteuse. They see the drum
kit and feel more comfortable, then they get into

it.'* Dana Bryant performs The Jackal's story in
a distant, ironic, humorous tone. The effect of
C.J.'s version is even stranger: slightly awkward
in her grey business suit, her gestures stiff, she
distances herself from the masculine myth of
the song. What remains is the virtuosity of the
words, their speed and rhythm. This performance, copying another, erases the legend and
keeps the pleasure of the text. *The West Wing*
embraces speed, heightens and incites it, but
never loses sight of the fact that it is not always
productive. My understanding of speed as a
tool does not ease the anxiety I feel hearing my
sister on the radio. Does working at a tormented
rhythm – the kind the media runs on – protect
you from torment itself? Can you shelter from
speed as you would shelter from the rain?

/ / /

When viewed from this perspective, speed
becomes a reflection of our vulnerabilities. I
wonder if it is better to plunge in or turn away
– slow down, play for time. This has become a

---

* 'The Lady speaks the Blues: you can see Dana
Bryant on MTV. So What? So she's a jazz poet. Joseph
Gallivan Reports', *The Independent*, 11 February 1993.

fashionable question. It seems to me that the human voice puts such questions on display because it reacts in real time, it responds, withdraws and has the power to deceive, unique among all the faculties. In these moments of pure reaction, the voice's inflections and intonations reveal the ways we engage, or refuse to engage, in the rush of conversations, decisions, displacements. I have noticed that three motifs, ones that often intersect, are uniquely vulnerable to being modified or affected by speed: relationships (which families, close relationships or affinities are formed by or resist speed?), bodies (how are they, or aren't they, made up of accelerations? How do they assimilate them, or not?) and knowledge (does going faster mean knowing how to do things better?). These three categories often overlap.

/ / /

I go to the medical appointment as if it were routine. The gynaecologist is away, and her replacement sees me. She has caught a cold from her daughter and can't shake my hand. She has my blood test results. She puts the paper in front of me. She circles two figures and explains that they are bad. From then on everything goes much too fast, the picture turns fuzzy and my attempts to slow down the conversation are completely unsuccessful. I'm too anxious to hear what she's saying except for a few phrases: 'It's going to be complicated', 'You might want to think about IVF'. I ask her for tissues. The printer seems to be working at full speed. I find myself in the waiting room again, then in the street, with a sheaf of referrals for further examinations in my hand. Later, when people ask for more details, to understand better, I won't be able to give any.

/ / /

In summer 2016, Sarah and Nans wrote, directed and acted in their first play, *Maintenant l'apocalypse*. The project was inspired by the diary kept by Eleanor Coppola during the shooting of *Apocalypse Now*. She was preparing to direct the film's 'making-of' documentary. The diary describes the titanic project, but also – and especially – its run of bad luck, the failures, the typhoons, the delays, the heart attacks, all the catastrophes that punctuated this legendary, cursed undertaking in the heart of the Philippines. Sarah says that while reading the book, her attention was caught not so much by the fascinating behind-the-scenes of the film nor by the couple navigating a monumental crisis, but rather by what the diary represents: a woman with no independent goals or desires working on a secret project, just for herself. Reading Eleanor, Sarah began to feel as though she were uncovering something deep and hidden: the idea that Eleanor desired catastrophe a little, as well as fearing it. Francis was too powerful, too mad, too rich. The relationship unravels as, like his characters, he pushes on deeper into the jungle. Perhaps standing at the edge of the abyss allows you to comprehend it. In order to reconstruct something of the various disasters described in the diary, Sarah and Nans play around twenty characters. As well as Eleanor there is Doug, who helps Eleanor film the making-of, and then the assistants, the actors, the script girl, the tiger tamer, Bunny Girl – two years of filming portrayed in this profusion of characters. Sarah and Nans embody more and more of them without ever changing costumes or scenery, switching from one character to another without warning. This is a mechanism which runs on acceleration. The project has an unstoppable force to it, all its trajectories melding together. This superposition gives a truer picture of the chaos than would a detailed and objective description of events. The play's speed matches the tempo of the emergencies we face in our lives. Whether we welcome this rhythm or suppress it, perhaps what Sarah is trying to do immunises us to it, like a vaccine.

/ / /

Sometimes my motifs (family/body/knowl-
edge) overlap. Italian writer Natalia Ginzburg
says that she writes very fast because her older
brothers were always telling her to stop talking
during meals when she was a child. She got
into the habit of saying what she wanted to
say as fast as possible, using as few words as
she could, for fear that the others would start
talking among themselves again and stop listening to her. Her book *Family Sayings* (*Lessico
famigliare*, 1963) is a good demonstration of
how the exchange of words in a family setting
sometimes imposes its own tempo. Some people
possess language, others manage to obtain it,
still more are unable to retain it. She explains
that writing this book was exactly like speaking:
'Scriverlo era per me del tutto come parlare'.
Her role as spectator and protagonist offers a
singular point of view from which she can perfectly record the density of conversations, their
cryptic, cacophonic nature, and interpret their
secrets. The dialogues which dominate *Family
Sayings* are innervated, connected to the idea
of speed, which can break out at any moment
without warning. Orality must always be able
to invite itself in and rush onto the page, just
as family life is shot through with speech, often

poorly timed (especially coming from the father figure). No protocols, no rules, no transitions: the discussions are anarchic. Here, therefore, speed is also a survival strategy in a sometimes-uncompromising family environment.

///

The aim of this book is to draw out the associations between fictional characters, real people, stories, affects and emotions. Some of these links, that is to say the transitions from one subject to another – transitions which are also relationships – sketched themselves out very quickly. But I was disappointed when I realised what a steep, craggy path I would have to climb. I would need to use writing, whose function it is to make connections, to reconstruct all the different pathways I had travelled so quickly alone. I wanted to preserve something of the initial speed, the speed at which we travel through dreams but also through emergencies, which had conjured up these objects in relation to one another. During the writing process, I also came to understand that this rhythm – if I managed to find it – would also let me sidestep the impassive, cold and detached kind of writing I most wanted to avoid. Speed encourages reckless-ness. I needed a method that would both disturb the mechanisms of certainty and validation and affirm its own plurality and incompleteness.

/ / /

People who know each other well talk fast together. Speed disrupts the normal course of familiarity, or else accelerates it. I am struck by this when I see old friends, for example. Over time they have built up a common language which needs no transitions. They pass from one subject to another as fast as lightning. If I haven't seen them for a while, I can end up lost in the middle of a conversation – they go too fast for me.

/ / /

Enrico leaves for Brussels to see Anne Waldman perform. He is researching the Beat Generation for an exhibition in the Pompidou Centre. I didn't know her writing before he introduced me to it. In 1975, Anne Waldman, who had then been directing the Bowery's Poetry Project for ten years, published *Fast Speaking Woman*, the long poem that would establish her reputation and which lists everything a woman who speaks fast is, or still is:

I'm the taxi woman
I'm the tactile woman
I'm the ductile woman
I'm the taciturn woman
I'm the fierce woman
I'm the Jupiter woman
I'm the tiger woman
I'm the woman with claws
I'm the woman with fangs
I'm the matinee woman
I'm the Neanderthal woman
I'm the decadent woman
I'm the opulent woman [...]*

A decade or more before this, Waldman had begun a writing practice which incorporated things she heard on the street, on the radio, snatches of conversation, fragments of the life pulsing through the Lower East Side: 'I was writing nightly, completely charged by the constant activity – artistic, political – of the Lower East Side environment... Use it! An immediacy and urgency took hold to write all waking and sleeping details down quickly – as witness, as

---

*Extract from 'Fast Speaking Woman', from *Fast Speaking Woman. Chants & Essays*, Pocket Poets Series No. 33, by Anne Waldman, City Lights Books: San Francisco, p.16 of the 1996 expanded edition.

eyeballer of phenomena – and accept whatever shape they took'.* Recording techniques
replace, stimulate or even accelerate writing:
speaking into a tape recorder, collecting sounds
and street noise, the conversations taking place
in New York apartments, overlapping voices. As
Director of the Poetry Project, Waldman turned
public readings into a medium of their own.
The *New Year's Marathon Readings* gather up
to 100 poets who each read for three minutes.
Waldman's own experiences of readings and
performances, hearing her own voice, gave
public readings a new importance for her: '"Performance" interested me in that it expanded
text off the page... I'd felt from my first reading
at St. Mark's church, where I sat, head bowed
to page, that the voice coming out of me was
only partial, and that I had a bigger sound to
exhibit and explore. A sound that I would literally "have to grow into".'† I keep in mind the
idea that our voices grow and transform with
us, that we shape and tame them. I see Anne
Waldman as a specialist, an expert on the voice.

---

* Quoted by Roxanne Power Hamilton, 'Take Everyone
to Heaven with Us: Anne Waldman's Poetry Cultures',
in *Impossible to Hold. Women and Culture in the 1960s*
(edited by Avital Bloch and Lauri Umansky), New York,
New York University Press, 2005.
† Ibid.

/ / /

We sang a lot when I was little, most notably a whole repertoire of revolutionary songs. We sometimes learned them phonetically, even though they were all collected in a classic 'cahier jaune'. One of the songs contained the line 'Le peuple aura ta peau' (The people will have your head). When we were children, a friend of mine heard it as 'Le peuple Ratapo' (The Ratapo people). The song became the tale of a strange people from a faraway land. Hearing is twice as fast as speech: the ear, too, creates shortcuts, all those fictional scenarios which are sparked by 'mishearing' a word. In short, an amateur understanding, a child's understanding, can modify flow and content without us even noticing our mistakes – which we get attached to and sometimes continue to hear years later.

/ / /

Howard Hawks 'composed' the dialogue of *His Girl Friday* (1940) to go as fast as possible since, according to him, talking pictures had 'slowed down films'. The characters are constantly interrupting one another. Hawks said that to create this effect you have to add words to the beginnings and ends of lines which will inevitably be 'covered up' by the next speaker. This superposition does not exist in real life; it is simply an effect of writing. Artificiality drives the film's vitalist energy, its singular vibration. Of course, speed drives the plot as well, especially the love story, but without ever tackling it head-on. Events move so fast that the two main characters never have the time to confess their love, and the tension of their careers becomes a substitute for the attraction between them. Love is expressed through work, and work offers just as many vibrational frequencies as love. The film's closest exchange to a declaration of love is probably this:

> Hildy: I thought you didn't love me.
> Walter: What were you thinking with?*

But speed is also the reason behind the profound melancholy which pervades *His Girl Friday* and especially its female protagonist. At the start of the film, Hildy (Rosalind Russell) has broken up with Walter (Cary Grant), the editor of the newspaper where she has been an ace reporter for years. Bruce, her new boyfriend, is

---

* *His Girl Friday*, directed by Howard Hawks, performances by Rosalind Russell and Cary Grant, Columbia Pictures, 1940.

a bland insurance broker from Albany. Bruce could never live life at the breakneck speed of journalism. He promises Hildy something different: tranquillity. But Hildy needs adrenaline, and Walter takes advantage of this to win her back with various schemes. It is speed, then, that dooms Hildy's relationship with Bruce: with him, life would go on without frisson, without suspense, with none of the intensity her job has always offered (the film is peppered with deadlines: articles to turn in, phones constantly ringing, a death sentence, Hildy and Bruce's wedding). Russell plays a woman consumed by her work in a time when most female film characters were housewives. But to pursue her passion, she has to choose, to settle on one path: 'She can't have it all.' Conscious of the fact that speed was the driving force behind her character, Russell reveals in her autobiography, *Life is a Banquet*,* that she secretly hired a screenwriter to rework her lines, which she found less funny and hard-hitting than Grant's.

/ / /

---

*Rosalind Russell and Chris Chase, *Life is a Banquet*, New York, Random House, 1977.

Two months after my first appointment, I begin going for further testing in clinics which get farther and farther away. I go to one of the appointments without having understood – had they explained it to me? – that it's for a perfusion MRI. I'm a little shocked. They put in the drip, I'm in a kind of hospital gown. There's a huge queue for the MRI, I have to wait. They sit me down with the IV in my arm in a room that must measure two square metres. Time goes by. A long time. I'm dizzy. I try to get up and fall to the ground. The cold tiles bring back memories of long-forgotten skiing holidays. They bring me round with sugar water, patting my cheeks, my legs in the air. They explain that it's time, it's my turn, I have to get into the machine, no time to lose. When the results come back, I hear the word 'endometriosis' applied to me for the first time. On the paper they give me is a note: 'Fainted during exam.'

///

Powell and Pressburger's film *A Matter of Life and Death* (1946) begins in space, among the planets of our solar system. We zoom in slowly on an Earth at war. It emerges gradually from above, enveloped by a layer of fog. We hear the crackle of radio messages, the sound of bombing, explosions, a Churchill speech. The film's opening scene is incandescent, drenched in red, following a call-and-response rhythm. An English pilot calls ground control from his flaming aeroplane. His parachute is gone, his co-pilot is gone. He will have to make an emergency landing; his chances of survival are slim. He wants to dictate his last thoughts to the young woman on the other end of the line. The connection is bad: 'Are you receiving me?', 'I cannot read you', 'Are you wounded?'. The operator and the pilot have a rushed conversation. He has time to learn her name, where she comes from. He recites a few stanzas of poetry to her, hastily tells her about himself. The voices are urgent, stifled by emotion, the faces filmed in extreme close-up. In a state of emergency, never having seen each other, they fall in love. Love at first hearing. In this scene, speed is synonymous with emergency. The bodies are separated but voices are posited as a survival technique, capable of forming new relationships.

///

Musician and feminist activist Kiran Gandhi (stage name Madame Gandhi, the ex-drummer of rapper M.I.A.) ran the London Marathon in April 2015 on the first day of her period, letting

the blood run down her legs. In a piece she later wrote about this, she would point out the role of language in our collective construction of taboo: 'It is the inability for someone to speak clearly and comfortably about their own bodies. It is feeling the need to apologize to someone else if they hear you speak about your period. It is whispering to ask a friend for a pad instead of being able to ask for one openly like you might be able to ask for a Band-Aid. It is keeping quiet about severe menstrual cramps at work, instead of being able to express honestly that you are in pain, the same way you might if you had a bad stomach ache from eating old food. It is not having access to language that makes you feel safe or normal when talking about your body, instead of awkward and uncomfortable... [N]ot having socially acceptable vocabulary for being able to talk about your own body comfortably is the most effective form of oppression. It prohibits women from being able to speak confidently about what is happening to them biologically.'*
Running the marathon, playing the drums, facing up to speed: these bodies in motion and

---

*Kiran Gandhi and Manjit K. Gill, 'The menstrual taboo in India and in the US: What does it look like, why does it exist?', *Thomson Reuters Foundation News*, 7 July 2016.

these questions of technique move me because
they confront things that are hidden – things
concerning 'what is happening to us biologically'
but also those surrounding medical discourse.

///

I discovered *Poto & Cabengo* (1978) while I was
participating in a project in Geneva about the
role of the essay in cinema. But I think it was
Mia who first told me about it, years ago. She
had seen the film in Vienna and brought back
the poster, which is still on the wall of her daughter's room: two little girls in gingham dresses are
holding hands, looking at the camera with mis-
chievous, troubled expressions. The language
of the twin girls Grace and Virginia Kennedy,
which Jean-Pierre Gorin documented in the
California suburb where they lived, sounds like
a sped-up recording, as though you had pressed
fast-forward while listening to an audiobook.
The film's opening is like an investigation. A
voiceover narrates news excerpts which intro-
duce the viewer to a unique human-interest
story: a pair of twins have developed a shared
language known only to themselves. What
Gorin discovers when he meets the twins and
spends time with them is that this language,
which at the time captivated both the press

and the psychiatric community, was the result of a singularly assimilated family vocabulary. Raised by an American father and a German mother who met at the end of the war, along with their maternal grandmother (who spoke no English), the girls were immersed in an improbable cocktail of languages that they were unable to untangle. Their gibberish – which Gorin will call a 'Creolised' language – is an attempt to meld their two native tongues, indicating that the family is a site where interaction is impossible. By the time Gorin meets them, the twins are already beginning to lose their language, trapped by the various methods put in place to make them 'conform'. Only vestiges remain. When I discuss it with her again, Mia says how sad the film really is. It is the story of a world, built by two little girls just for themselves, which is disappearing. A world in which they seemed so much more at ease, independent and happy. The speed of their language seems to protect their secret. It has nothing to do here with performance or efficiency. It is more like a shield, protecting them from the outside world.

///

The speed of speeches, stories and orders manifests our fears and makes them palpable. It prevents us from sorting intelligently through the constant background noise of rumours, ambiances, implications and what people say to us. This noise transmits our fears, lending them more weight and reality with each passing day. But speed is also what allows us to escape, to repatriate ourselves, and we can therefore more broadly make use of it, become sensitive to it, come to need it.

///

During the series of events Teresa and I organised about Laura Mulvey in Paris in April 2018, we planned an evening of film showings at the Le Grand Action cinema. We had asked the English artist Lucy Reynolds to organise something for the occasion and very soon she suggested a reading of Mulvey's writings: *A Feminist Chorus*. She proposed we bring together three different groups – which she called the *readers*, the *makers* and the *viewers* – to do the reading. Teresa and I recruited the members of each group in Paris. We contacted female students, friends, filmmakers and artists. Lucy wrote to them: 'It is important to stress that a strong element of *A Feminist Chorus* – in the different forms it has taken since 2014 – is that it is not rehearsed and is not about professionalised singing (though you are very welcome to sing your chosen extract if you would like to!) but about creating a collective voice and a cacophony of feminist sound. It would be good for us to all meet together prior to the chorus – and I will be there to cue you in to start speaking – but it's important that it is a spontaneous event where the agency is with you, with Laura's texts as a score running through.' So Katinka, Isabelle, Manon, Nicole, Jackie, Raquel, Sophie, Pascaline, Rubis, Adèle, Émilie, Céline, Maria, Charlotte, Chloé, Hélène, Marcelline, Wagner, Martina, Caroline, Nora and more met at the cinema for the event about Laura Mulvey that Saturday, extracts in hand. Nothing had been rehearsed, and we had only communicated by email. Lucy met the women in the foyer and explained to each group how the readings would be organised. At various points before or after the films, while the lights were out, they would take out their mobile phones to use as torches, stand up, and read in the dark, in English and French, before sitting down again. Their voices mingling. Cacophony is a technique in and of itself, which defies the expectation of readability: the meaning of the words disappears, but the sight of all these women standing, mixing their voices in the dark, their faces flickering in the cinema, evokes an emotion that only improvisation and rapidity can provide.

It is no easy task to find ways to include our
multiple voices within the various texts we
create – in film, poetry, feminist theory... I feel
it even now, writing this piece when I gave it
talking and reading, talking spontaneously,
using familiar academic speech now and then,
'talking the talk' – using black vernacular
speech, the intimate sounds and gestures
I normally save for family and loved ones.
Private speech in public discourse, intimate
intervention, making another text, a space
that enables me to recover all that I am in
language, I find so many gaps, absences
in this written text. To cite them at least
is to let the reader know something has
been missed, or remains there hinted at
by words – there in the deep structure.

bell hooks
'Choosing the Margin as a Space
of Radical Openness'

6. IRRITATION

Becoming a heroine

Translated by Jennifer Higgins

Bordeaux: I cross the Place Saint-Michel in the rain, listening to Nathalie Quintane on France Culture. She thinks we need to get over the idea that literature is there to save us, to heal or repair us: 'As the world falls flat on its face and we become increasingly troubled, unsettled, worried, nervous and stressed [...], literature, just like self-help and self-coaching books, is seen as a personal, private aid to feeling better. [...] I'm not saying that can't be one of its roles. [...] But I think it shouldn't just be that. [...] Being enclosed in a kind of contemplative, consolatory meditation kills: it kills us and it kills literature too.'* Hearing her slightly tense, acerbic voice, I backtrack to the start of my research. The idea of irritation as a motif came to me when I was thinking about her books and the effects they produce. The subjects she tackles and the atmospheres she creates allow

---

* 'Trahissons la littérature pour qu'enfin elle vive', *Par les temps qui courent*, Marie Richeux, France Culture, 29 March 2018.

Nathalie Quintane to construct a form that is irritated, located between contained anger and a kind of humour or irony that works at the surface of the sentence itself. When this idea is put to work, the result is an apt depiction of the contemporary situation: unsatisfying and rather brooding, treading water but trying to make something out of that stasis. I like this translation of annoyance into a literary form. Irritation is the subject of some of Nathalie Quintane's work, as is the way in which the rough edges of spoken language impinge on the regularity of the written word. In 2006, Quintane was interviewed about her book *Cavale* (meaning 'escape'). The journalist asks her if 'escape' is a 'solution to depression'. She answers: 'No, if there is an element of escape then, as I've said, it's more that ideas are escaping. But yes, if we want to escape in the literal sense, it might also be because our ideas are escaping. It's a response to the current atmosphere, which everyone talks about but can't pin down'. She's asked if she's referring to the 'current political situation'. 'Er, no, mine. I mean, it comes from the bizarre conversations I sometimes have with my friends about all this. We've turned forty, we're well educated, but sometimes it feels worse than the endless wrangling of the Villepin-Sarkozy business. It's like a complete mental swamp. A struggle to think through the before, the after, the during. But I think it's a time that suits me, in terms of ideas escaping. I recognise this fog of confusion, because it's something that has dogged me for years. Nothing's certain.'*

///

Several times in my professional life I've thought I should learn to swallow my anger. I observe and experiment with the extent to which my publicly manifested anger is difficult, even impossible, for people to accept. And I feel isolated by it, separated. To swallow: 'Swallow one's feelings', 'Stifle or repress', 'Swallow one's saliva (due to emotion, anxiety or hesitation)', but especially, 'Send back down the throat'.

///

'A response to the current atmosphere', Quin-tane says. Irritation is formless but it makes us

* Eric Loret, 'De la suite dans les idées fixes', *Libération*, cahier Livres, Paris, 11 May 2006. Interview transcribed in Alain Farah's PhD in modern writing and literary studies entitled *La Possibilité du choc. Invention littéraire et résistance politique dans les oeuvres d'Olivier Cadiot and Nathalie Quintane*, August 2009, University of Quebec in Montréal.

itch. It's always making its presence felt, establishing itself inside us. Swallowed down and interiorised, it struggles to find its voice. Even though anger provides an immediate, effective outlet, I'm choosing irritation here – less fertile, maybe, but more unifying. More muted and odourless, it infects like a virus. Irritation, it seems to me, is more shareable than anger.

/ / /

In the 1990s, the artist Carolee Schneemann was interviewed by Alexandra Juhasz, who was investigating the link between feminist convictions and the media. The interview inevitably spills over into other topics, and ends up implying that irritation is not completely separate from humour.

Alexandra Juhasz: I would like you to talk about the legacy of your work. I want to know what we owe you.

Carolee Schneemann: You owe me the vulva. You owe me the concept of vulvic space. You owe me bestiality. You owe me the love of the presence of the cat as a powerful companion and energy. You owe me heterosexual pleasure and the depiction of that pleasure. And you owe me thirty years of lost work that's never been seen. That's what you all owe me. [...] I'm glad you've asked. Nobody has ever asked me. And you can see I'm fuming underneath.

A. J.: Well it's a history of anger and frustration. It's also a history of loss.

C. S.: Tremendous loss. Personal loss. Partnership loss: the underlying secret conflict in my lovers between pleasure and excitement and equity of being with an artist and their final decision always to become a father and have a traditional marriage. That's a big layer of loss. Of course, we lose everything sooner or later, but one would prefer later.

A. J.: And anger...

C. S.: Well anger always has to go with humour and pleasure. Anger has to be honed; with your biggest iron mallet you take the anger and you go at it long enough so that you can tune it. It has to become funny and outrageous and made back into something aesthetic. It's not good enough on its own. But it's good.*

---

*In *Women of Vision, Histories in Feminist Film and Video,* ed. Alexandra Juhasz, Minneapolis, London, University of Minnesota Press, 2001. In *Women of*

/ / /

Benjamin lends me *La Voix endeuillée* (*The Mourning Voice*) by the historian Nicole Loraux, in which she explains how, in ancient cities, it was necessary to forget conflict in order for the city to function properly.* It was only by swallowing potential sources of conflict that were constantly lapping at the edges of society that the social contract could be maintained. However, Electra's mourning voice is one of those that is raised and refuses to stick to that contract. These figures, women of antiquity who carry their anger everywhere with them, fascinate me. Electra's anger is a nuisance – even the chorus tell her so: her mourning is excessive, her lamentation is too intransigent: 'You are not the

Vision, the writer and theorist of media production Alexandra Juhasz transcribes the voices of twenty-one women who are linked to her research into feminism and the media in different ways. Activists, artists, educators, film distributors, critics, researchers: all considered how their techniques and savoir-faire could help them describe their political, artistic and professional convictions. The interviews were recorded between 1995 and 1996 as part of the production of a documentary (completed in 1998).
* *La Voix endeuillée*, Gallimard, 1999. *The Mourning Voice: An Essay on Greek Tragedy*, Nicole Loraux. Translated from the French by Elizabeth Trapnell Rawlings. Cornell University Press. 2002.

only mortal to have known pain.' Her 'rejection of amnesty' sticks in my mind. Nicole Loraux's exploration of the concept of 'unending' sets out the idea of the permanence of anger within multiple timeframes and scenarios: 'a constructive repetition in an unbroken continuity'. The tragic heroines believe in this perpetuation, this fixation with time beyond time, and that is what constitutes their madness. Their incantations become a lamentation evoking something 'unending': a form of negativity from which they refuse to emerge, and with which women seem to be more familiar than anyone.

///

I decide to give a place to this slightly suppressed verbal combustion, which struggles to find its form and often fizzles out. I begin to collect moments when conversations catch fire. Cinema and recent contemporary fiction provide me with interesting examples. But once you start to pay attention, everyday life is literally overflowing with these situations, which are much more striking than 'examples' I might find, and full of details, textures, words and gestures that make up irritation. My telephone conversations with friends remain the best place to observe it. These exchanges are attempts to catch hold of daily lives that are lived at unbelievable speed: accounts of trying to juggle careers, romantic situations, travel, children, home life – all at once. Several times I've put the phone down and regretted not having recorded all these conversations. They are the most fully developed image of lives shot through with annoyance, irritation and disappointments, and they manage to turn things around with humour, rejecting the seemingly inevitable. I often have the sense that these female characters, who are very real and all around me, are true heroines, champions of organisation as much as of chaos, and that their ability to articulate and join up these scattered experiences has a literary quality. The common factor in all the episodes is irritation, which roughens up transitions and disrupts and complicates any simple, languid acceptance of difficulty. Irritation makes these women demanding, caustic and angry, ready to hold people to account. It's this capacity to dramatise that interests me, because it serves to create a narrative. I draw the temporary conclusion that irritation makes heroines of us.

/ / /

I remember that once, after having had a particularly bad cold, I developed a terrible cough which lasted for weeks. It was a scratchy cough, an irritation of the throat. Particularly active at night, it would come and lodge itself in my sleep, waking me in the middle of a dream. But I wasn't the only one it woke, and soon I was put into quarantine, consigned to a more distant bedroom where my irritation wouldn't disturb anyone else. Coughing as an artistic motif had been on my mind a long time earlier, when I was writing about a film by Peter Watkins, *Edvard Munch* (1974).* There, coughing is used as the physical and audible manifestation of the illness that is ravaging Munch's entourage – tuberculosis. Coughing suddenly erupts at the end of a shot or a sentence, sometimes making the camera itself shake: a harbinger of death. It creeps into the most mundane activities. Katherine Mansfield also seems to have suffered from night-time coughing: 'I seem to spend half of my life arriving at strange hotels. The strange door shuts upon the stranger, and then I slip down in the sheets. Waiting for the shadows to come out of the corners and spin their slow, slow web over the Ugliest Wallpaper of All... The man in the room next to mine has the same complaint as I. When I wake in the night I hear

---

*In French this film is known as *Edvard Munch, la danse de la vie* (*Edvard Munch, the Dance of Life*).

him turning. And then he coughs. And after a silence I cough. And he coughs again. This goes on for a long time. Until I feel we are like two roosters calling each other at false dawns. From far-away hidden farms.'*

///

The actor Jeanne Balibar was interviewed on the radio about a play in which she was starring, *La Dame aux Camélias*, adapted from the novel by Alexandre Dumas: 'You could say that *La Dame aux Camélias* isn't a very exciting text in literary terms, and politically it's pretty revolting, but it is interesting in that it's symptomatic of France in 1848, when it was written. And actually all of Marguerite's coughing fits are also, in a way, the revolutionary spasms shaking the country that year. In 1848, France went from one revolution to another, from one revolutionary uprising to the next, so there's this sort of French social body trying to bring about liberty and egality and fraternity, but never succeeding. And in a way that's also Marguerite Gauthier.'†

---

*Quoted by Susan Sontag in *Illness as Metaphor* (1977), New York, Farrar, Strauss and Giroux.
† Interview with Jeanne Balibar, *La Grande table*, by Caroline Broué, France Culture, 10 January 2012.

/ / /

In February 2017, Joan sends me a link to a
poem, 'Nasty Women', written and performed
by Nina Donovan (a nineteen-year-old sociology
student in Franklin, Tennessee) in response to
Trump calling Hillary Clinton a nasty woman
during their presidential debate. She's being
filmed on a phone, and we see her, small and
slight, dressed in an orange jumper and worn
jeans, walking up to a microphone in the
middle of the stage. A few fans shout encour-
agement. Then she starts to recite her poem.
Her voice is clear and quite penetrating, and
her hands move as she speaks. She stands
very straight and her voice doesn't waver. As
she recites, it's also as though she were talking
to us, very simply, as though she were telling
us a story. But the tone intensifies, the rhythm
is incredible, the story takes off, and references to Trump's America – its violence, its
racism, its worsening inequality – make her
thin voice a vehicle for unbounded irritation.
The text was recited again by Ashley Judd at
the Women's March on 21 January 2017, but
there's no comparison. Nina Donovan's voice
resonates with astonishing power. Like the
voice of Emma Gonzales, who was born in 1999
and escaped from the high school shooting in

Parkland, Florida in February 2018. I often talk with Joan about these very young women in front of microphones, so serious and vehement. Like me, Joan teaches in an art school and observes her female students carefully, noticing what makes them angry, what spurs them to action.

///

'Greek women of the archaic and classical periods were not encouraged to pour forth unregulated cries of any kind within the civic space of the *polis* or within earshot of men. Indeed masculinity in such a culture defines itself by its different use of sound. Verbal continence is an essential feature of the masculine virtue of *sophrosyne* ('prudence, soundness of mind, moderation, temperance, self-control') that organizes most patriarchal thinking on ethical or emotional matters. [...] In general, the women of classical literature are a species given to disorderly and uncontrolled outflow of sound – to shrieking, wailing, sobbing, shrill lament, loud laughter, screams of pain or of pleasure and eruptions of raw emotion in general. As Euripides puts it [in *Andromache*], "For it is woman's inborn pleasure always to have her current emotions coming up to her mouth and out through her tongue".'*

/ / /

Holly, one of the sisters in Woody Allen's *Hannah and Her Sisters* (1986), is an actor. She is constantly looking for solutions, in life and in work. For a while, she goes into business with her friend April, and together they set up the 'Stanislavski Catering Company', providing food at cocktail parties. At one particular party, Holly and April meet David Tolchin – an architect and opera lover – who comes into the kitchen for a snack. He's intelligent and self-assured, slightly vulgar and unselfconscious. Both women are attracted to him straight away. They ask him what he does, he asks them if they're really interested, and when they say they want to know more, he asks them what time they finish work. The film then cuts to a shot of the three characters in a car, in front of a building that David has recently built. There follows an improbable exchange about architecture – improbable in that it serves as a façade masking the true intentions of the sequence. As often with Woody

*Anne Carson, 'The Gender of Sound', in *Glass, Irony and God.*

Allen, this conversation about broad cultural ideas is an excuse for verbal jousting, fiery monologues and stereotypical exchanges – flashy small-talk underpinning social intercourse that is based on seduction. After the discussion in the car, the architect takes the young women to see his favourite buildings in New York, once again at their request. This section of the film, ostentatious and grandiloquent, underscored by Puccini's *Madame Butterfly*, is made in the image of the male character. After this 'guided tour', the three find themselves standing next to Tolchin's car; he must now decide which of the women he will drop home first. It is decided that it will be Holly, as she lives in Chelsea. Her hopes of spending some time alone with Tolchin are shattered. Sitting in the passenger seat, we hear her comments on what has just happened in a voiceover: she describes her jealousy of April, who has come off better and who knew what to say and when to say it. Strangely, Woody Allen once again chooses Puccini as the soundtrack for Holly's confession. Is it revenge against the previous sequence, so violently taken hostage by the architect's words and certitudes? Holly's doubts and self-pity are funny in the way they show how she perceives herself, but they also portray an irritation that everything has conspired to create. This irritation has no clear object: Holly resents herself as much as she resents other people. Her voice deconstructs the whole of the scene we've just witnessed: she is its critical commentary, and the commentary is hostile. Holly's irritated voice encapsulates feminine failure, a woman caught in the snare of her own doubts. But the sequence also enacts a process of reappropriation through music: a piece that has been 'tarnished' by unthinking self-sufficiency takes on a new, courageous tonality. The woman's irony contradicts the architect's assuredness: he had the upper hand in the preceding images, but she takes revenge in the secrecy of her interior monologue. The alternative routes that she constructs are so many stratagems to resist the masculine domination she has just been subjected to. Her irritation is ultimately joyful.

/ / /

In April 2016, Joan points out something else to me: the maiden speech (*maiden* speech!) given by her Scottish heroine, Mhairi Black. Born in 1994, Black was, at 20, the youngest person ever to be elected to parliament, as an MP for the Scottish National Party. She is known for her frank, forceful speeches: questioned on her own experience of coming out, she replied, 'I've

175

never been in.' On 7 March 2018, she revealed the torrent of insults she regularly receives by email, reading some out loud in parliament, notes in hand. Her accent, which makes her speeches completely incomprehensible to me, heightens my pleasure in listening to her. For me, it becomes synonymous with her irritation.

///

The following speech is delivered straight to camera by Jane Fonda in *Tout va bien* (1974), a film by Jean-Luc Godard, made in the wake of the events of May 1968. Fonda's character is an American reporter based in France, and she says the words in English but they are then dubbed into French, also by Fonda. So here we need to imagine Jane Fonda's crystal-clear French accent. She's being interviewed, and reveals the doubts she has as a journalist, and her difficulty in finding the right way to describe what she wants to talk about: 'I'm really sick of it. If this carries on, the same thing's going to happen every week. Yes, I've been working at American Broadcasting in Paris for nearly three and a half years now. At the beginning I was in the culture department – literature, cinema, different things. Anyway, I was bored stiff doing all that. I moved over into politics after May '68.

Not completely, actually – they let me have a foot in each department. What happened was that they were completely taken by surprise by May. And I exploited that. It worked for them. [...] I suggested investigations. It makes no sense, because now I fight each week to get them to admit that we absolutely must talk about such and such a thing, and at the same time I know full well that I'm incapable of writing it. For a week I work like crazy on a particular subject and I get nowhere. Maybe it's a question of style. I don't know if you're aware, but there's a house style. Listen to the programmes, and you really get the feeling that the same person wrote them all. Well, I can see that to talk about the things I want to talk about, that style's useless. [...] It comes from the things themselves, as though they made you write or speak in a different way. Anyway, I don't know. The more I think about it the less I feel I understand what's happening. The things in France I'm interested in are becoming completely opaque to me. I'm an American correspondent in France who doesn't correspond to anything at all!'

///

According to Sianne Ngai, who teaches literature at the University of Chicago, irritation

should be classified as a form of 'inappropriate'
or inadequate anger that can't be traced back
to a specific occasion or object. She links irritation to a mood or atmosphere rather than an
emotion. Irritation, simultaneously excessive
and lacking, is like Holly doing her very best
not to identify the exact cause of her irritation. It seems to overflow and attach itself to
the first thing that will submit to it. In terms of
its proportion and its object, it's never exactly
'well placed'. But Sianne Ngai's analysis of irritation is invaluable because she focuses on its
physical, bodily aspect: 'Whether "irritation" is
defined as an emotional or physical experience,
synonyms for it tend to apply equally to psychic
life *and* life at the level of the body – and particularly to its surfaces or skin. In addition to
"inflammation," "rawness," and "chafing," for
example, "irritation" qua "soreness" also sig-
nifies "hypersensitivity," "susceptibility," and
"tenderness," words with explicitly affective
dimensions easily turned, as we have seen,
into signifiers of social distinction in the late
nineteenth-century discourse of "nerves".* The
irritation that interests me isn't limited to the
shifting, annoyed, reactive inflections of the

---

*Sianne Ngai, *Ugly Feelings*, Cambridge, London,
Harvard University Press, 2005.

voice. It involves bodies, which often carry the marks of these transformations. The physical hypersensitivity highlighted by Sianne Ngai points back in time to the nineteenth-century concept of 'nerves', and the cultural script that laid the blame for toxic hysteria firmly at the door of women: all that emerges in irritation.

///

I read an article in *Libération* about Marianne Faithfull – her husky voice and her performance of 'Sister Morphine', a song she co-wrote with Mick Jagger and Keith Richards in 1969 when she was 23, before she ever touched heroin, which she would end up using until she was 40. Eventually, having come off the drug in hospital, she rediscovered real life and all its sensations. She suffered terrible toothache for weeks but didn't complain, convinced that pain was normal in a life without drugs. This misunderstanding led to her having open surgery on her jaw. In this instance it was pain, perceived as a mere irritation, that she bravely managed to swallow down.

///

Among my podcasts I come across a piece written
and read by Zadie Smith for the *New Yorker*.
Billie Holiday is talking to herself in 1957, two
years before her death; she is laid low by debts,
drugs and alcohol. It is said that these had
begun to affect her voice as early as the 1940s:
her diction was blurred, as was her sense of
rhythm, and her tone became rougher, huskier.
Zadie Smith's piece doesn't touch on this supposed damage, positioning itself elsewhere. I'm
interested in the way it transcribes an interior
voice, because Holiday is a singer, a black voice
(in her introduction, Smith describes this voice
as caught between 'delight and pain'), and also
it's quite a vindictive monologue, shot through
with annoyance – Holiday seems furious. This
fury is due, among other things, to the way
people talk about her voice: 'All the downtown
collectors and the white ladies in their own
fancy furs love to talk about your phrasing –
it's the fashion to talk about your phrasing
– but what sounds like a revolution to others
is simple common sense to you. All respect to
Ella, all respect to Sarah, but when those gals
open their mouths to sing, well, to you it's like
someone just opened a brand-new Frigidaire. A
chill comes over you. And you just can't do it
like that. Won't. It's obvious to you that a voice
has the same work to do, musically speaking, as

the sax or the trumpet or the piano. A voice has got to feel its way in. Who the hell doesn't know that?'* In 'Speaking in Tongues', a lecture delivered in 2008 at the New York Public Library,† Smith delves deep into her own relationship with language: dialects, slang and accents define the characters in her novels almost more than anything else. She talks about the way in which her 'English voice' came to her late, at university. It's a cultured voice, different from her original one, and the shift meant that she blended intonations and registers as she gradually lost the London accent of her youth. This period of her life, when she was double, voiced by multiple ways of speaking, was decisive for her.

///

Valerie Solanas is famous for her *SCUM Manifesto*, a 1967 feminist polemic published in New York, and for having shot Andy Warhol. Avital Ronell took up the figure of Solanas in

---

*Zadie Smith, 'Crazy They Call Me', *The New Yorker*, 6 March 2017.
†Zadie Smith, 'Speaking in Tongues', *The New York Review of Books*, 26 February 2009.

a venomous essay that asks an important question about irritation: can it make the leap from idea to action, as when Valerie goes from a written manifesto to a gun? There's (patriarchal) authority to be smashed, there are barriers to flatten – these things scratch away at us, irritate us, but when do they make us act, more than just through words? 'For Valerie, something was unleashed, something happened,' Ronell writes. This is the opening of her essay: 'More than anything else, Valerie Solanas wanted to write. Being unable to distribute her work, she took aim at metonyms of her avowed targets. But I'm getting ahead of myself. Let's go back in time and get a sense of Valerie Solanas and the non-place that she consistently occupied. Barely representable or representative, she was a blot, a spectre at the margins of extremist writing. Her writing was full of irony, trained on the real; confined within the cage of parasitic expression, she adopted the language of a scourge, plugging into a certain kind of discourse that plays devil's advocate while also resembling a discourse inciting hatred that is almost racial. [...] If you are categorised as a woman, your shrieking could be interpreted as one of a range of trifling strategies – diatribe, recrimination, harassment, gossip, and incompetence, which have been so useful, historically, in de-valuing or labelling women's discourse'.*

/ / /

Irritation, then, is a force – a narrative, activist, literary force, which makes every woman a potential heroine if we accept parasitic logic rather than maintaining a lazy status quo. It's a force that prompts Nathalie Quintane, again on France Culture, to say that the scent of flowers in Proust is very nice, but what do we do with it? 'Yes,' she explains, 'the scent of flowers is important, God knows we need the scent of flowers and the hum of insects – especially as they're all being wiped out all over the place – that is interesting, but let's not leave it at that. Let's not settle for experiencing the sensory world around us a bit more, a bit better, a bit more subtly. This sensory world is being wiped out, so we're going to need to use Proust in a way that goes beyond just "let's taste the beauty of the world for ourselves". Beauty isn't always going to be enough.'

---

* Avital Ronell, 'Rétribution indirecte: les buts de Valerie Solanas', in *Lignes de Front*, Paris, Stock, translated [into French] by Daniel Loayza.

///

My stays in Bordeaux were underpinned by a precarious housing situation. We were on a never-ending hunt for somewhere to live, with short periods of remission followed by abrupt crises because solutions suddenly became scarce. Madeleine, who taught in the same university as I did, went through all these episodes with me, and we'd try to fit in appointments around our teaching timetables. Sometimes this caused disappointments or misunderstandings. One evening, we were on the train home together when we discovered this voicemail left by an estate agent with whom we'd been trying to arrange to visit a flat. Her endless monologue manages not to mention the reasons for our exchanges despite its great length, but it overflows with irritation, and conjures up a possible image of our stays in Bordeaux: 'Yes, hello Madeleine, well listen, it's Nathalie. I'm a bit deeply shocked by your behaviour because yesterday we did discuss at length. I explained my priorities a little bit. You were very insistent. Seeing as how you're starting up again in January and you were leaving for Paris this evening. Anyway, I'm not going through the whole conversation again. I think you remember it as well as I can. And I have to say that, er, yes, it was quite an unpleasant surprise because I did make arrangements for you. And then, no reply. Just a text to tell me... Well anyway. I just think there's a lack of respect. I mean I appreciate, I'm the first to say, no problem. We all have complicated lives, meetings, this and that, commitments, we're all in the same boat in that way. But I'm rather disappointed, yes, by your way of going about things, you see. In any case, er, listen, as I said, I'm free now. Otherwise it'll be in the evening. So there you go, Madeleine. I got the feeling you were a respectful person, speaking for two... for three people in total, you seemed, you know, responsible, and everything. And I can see, well in any case it's basically par for the course in my profession, I see things you wouldn't believe. And you can't judge a book by its cover, Madeleine. Well okay you've got my number. You know what to do or what not to do. Because in the end sticking your head in the sand is an old trick, people not taking responsibility for their actions. In any case I look forward to a call from you. We all make mistakes. But it's also good to know when to say sorry and not take people for you know, my time's precious too, Madeleine, very precious. I hope you have an excellent Christmas, and I mean that. I imagine you ran into all sorts of unforeseen problems there, but I'd still have preferred to actually hear your voice over the phone, just as a matter of basic courtesy. There you go, Madeleine, that's genuinely what I think. I'm a straightforward, sincere person, I always say things as they are and it doesn't mean that two seconds later life can't go on and everybody has the right to change. But I'd have really appreciated a call from you. I hope you have an excellent Christmas, as I said, you and your colleagues'. What to do with a block of words like that, when it arrives in your ears at the end of the day, after all the interruptions, the gasps for breath, the overflowings, accelerations and irritations that you've got through as best you can? What to do with this unknown voice that insinuates itself, sets up camp, and takes the time to set out a state of mind, such a raw mood? Perhaps one way would be to acknowledge its literary and narrative power; we could look to the flux of the everyday, to the people who surround us or whose words we decide to listen to, for the richest store of accounts and stories, and for our desire to unpick them.

In March 2019, I take a few days away in London with Enrico to see the Tate Modern's Dorothea Tanning retrospective. I have a collection of images of her paintings, gathered online, showing female figures stepping into books. Often presented as if they were doors lying half-open, these books look like very abstract volumes, ensconced in inscrutable landscapes. The figures express something of my own investigations, of the starting points that allow me to situate myself: I, too, steal inside books, and I open doors. I picture myself wearing those long dresses, turning pages and slipping inside to join stories that always launch me on journeys to brand-new continents. For some time now, I've been using these images in my presentations, in speeches, to classes and at conferences. This way, my voice can re-energise Tanning's doors and books. With these images for a backdrop, I describe my working method. This lets me articulate where I'm speaking from – I try to avoid those moments when knowledge and understanding seem to arrive from very far away or even out of nowhere.

It's very rare that we know precisely who's speaking when people start to speak. A few years ago, Jean-Philippe told me about an American independent radio station, WFMU, that he used to tune in to, for a programme called 'This is the Modern World' hosted by DJ Trouble. He said that every time she comes on air – for DJ Trouble is a woman – she introduces herself with: 'Hello, I'm Trouble.' I think back to those female characters in the 1940s American comedies; to my favourite stars, Katherine Hepburn and Irene Dunne: their main function is to turn up and wreak mischief in the orderly lives of rather square young men, to disrupt their silky-smooth progress. By blowing in some contrary winds – and on occasion it's a veritable hurricane that batters the unsuspecting characters – they disrupt the dreary patterns these men have settled into.

In the 'modern' world of DJ Trouble – in our world, that is, trouble is the first to speak, she takes the mic before anything else, even before the first track is played. And trouble is always figured as a person – a woman, but it (or she) no longer requires a script or confinement to the twists and turns of a story. Trouble is the situation we find ourselves in, with which we have to make our peace – *Staying with the Trouble*, as Donna Haraway puts it. 'Hello, I'm Trouble': the words' weight depends above all on the voice that carries them. This weight goes far beyond any meaning we can impute to the phrase: for it to be *vocally* 'active', it must belong to someone; it must appear in a particular context; and it must define a territory. It's the combination of these factors, their yoking together which, in this particular case, brings trouble to the table. In this way, the words fill out with a texture that only lived, perceived experience can offer. Without it, they drift. So, voices offer me a way through, an exit route: from the words alone, to the ways they come to life in specific situations.

I'm listening to the distinct and limpid voice of philosopher Vinciane Despret discussing her new book about birds, on Radio France Culture. 'I'm reminded', she says, 'of a comment by my doctoral student Thibault de Meyer [...] He'd read a book on the potency of sounds by Salomé Voegelin. It led him to ask how sound affects our relationship to the world. Actually, when we're working on a visual plain, we're in the realm of certainty, where "seeing is believing" and other dicta like that pertain. Whereas with a sound, you have the creation of a mystery. You don't necessarily know where it's coming from, you don't know who produced it. Thibault went on to say that the sound prompts you to go and see, to go further. It sends you on a quest. [...] The quest for sounds is a quest born of curiosity that respects the fact we don't know everything, we don't have access to everything.'* I happen to be listening while drawing up the timetable of sessions I will offer my students at the Beaux-Arts school in Paris. I want them to read a short story, 'Sur', by Ursula K. Le Guin, in which, in the early 1900s, a group of women goes secretly in search of the South Pole – secretly, because no one will ever know their expedition took place: they intend to leave no trace at all. The journey is to form the heart of the women's experience; laurels and trophies hold no interest for them. After the first iceberg encounters, settling in, training and sledging sorties for reconnaissance, they set out on their austral expedition at last. In the midst of the cold and darkness, they begin to sing:

> That 'night' – of course there was no real
> darkness – we were all nine together in the
> heart of the level plain of ice. It was the
> fifteenth of November, Dolores's birthday. We

---

*Vinciane Despret, a guest on the programme 'La Grande table des idées' ('The round table of ideas') with Olivia Gesbert, 3 October 2019.

celebrated by putting eight ounces of pisco
in the hot chocolate and became very merry.
We sang. It is strange now to remember
how thin our voices sounded in that great
silence. It was overcast, white weather,
without shadows and without visible horizon
or any feature to break the level; there was
nothing to see at all. We had come to that
white place on the map, that void, and there
we flew and sang like sparrows.*

There was nothing to see on their expedition –
but everything to hear. So, while I'm finishing
the project of this book, Despret's robins and Le
Guin's sparrows work on me much as the birds
do in Disney's *Cinderella*, secretly constructing
Cinderella's dress so that, thanks to them, she
can go to the ball.

After the Tanning exhibition and before catching the train back to Paris, we just have time
to visit the Freud Museum. We take the underground. A strange feeling begins to grow on me,
which it takes me a while to put my finger on.
The London underground is very narrow. I am
seven months pregnant and I think at first that
my discomfort is due to feeling a little crowded-
in, in a jam-packed tube train. But actually, it's

---

*Ursula K. Le Guin, 'Sur', 1967.

something else and I realise what as I observe the people around me. There isn't another woman to be seen anywhere. The train is, literally, filled with male passengers. The situation is implausible. So implausible that I take a ridiculously long time to speak up and demand Enrico's corroboration that I'm not seeing things. We change trains and our explanation arrives at the next platform: a football match is to kick off in half an hour – Arsenal vs. Tottenham. The underground is filled with the supporters. Groups of friends, fathers and sons, a crowd that's oddly short on fever, generally quiet but incredibly present and arresting. A little disorientated, I examine these people temporarily bereft of women and apparently handling their absence, their lack, so well. More than anything, I'm struck by their silence; I recall this scene as if someone had cut off the sound: a voiceless society. As we go on our way, in these tube trains that seem to function perfectly well ferrying great rafts of unperturbed supporters, without a word, without birdsong, without headwinds, I think… what tedium!

Translated by Sophie Lewis

• Thanks & acknowledgments •

It is in the company of my friend and publisher Thomas Boutoux, that this book found its definitive shape.

Thanks to Lise Wajeman, an unreplaceable person to speak to; for supporting me through my hesitations with such gentleness.

Their stories are interspersed through *Zizanies*. By order of appearance, thanks to: Solenn Morel, Benjamin Thorel, Benjamin Valenza, Armand Jalut, Gabriel Rosenman, Lila Pinell, Enrico Camporesi, Gaëlle Obiégly, Katinka Bock, Alexia Caunille, Maïder Fortuné, Nora Barbier, Hugo Benayoun Bost, François Piron, Eva Helft, Lola Schulmann, Fanny Schulmann, Jonathan Pouthier, Sarah Le Picard, Nans Laborde Jourdaa, Mia Hansen-Løve, Teresa Castro, Joan Ayrton, Madeleine Montaigne, Jean-Philippe Antoine.

Parts of this book started with conferences or published pieces. For these work opportunities and the exchanges they fostered, thanks to: Bruno Nassim Aboudrar, François Aubart, Alexandra Baudelot, Erik Bullot, Jeanne Gailhoustet, Danièle Hibon,

Apostolos Lampropoulos, Barbara Le Maître, Marcella Lista, Dario Marchiori, Valérie Mréjen, Elena Papadopoulos, Laura Preston, Lúcia Ramos Monteiro, Bertrand Schefer, Mathilde Villeneuve.

For their help and support, all my thanks to: Patricia Falguières, David Gilberg, Germain Filoche, Marie Muracciole, Didier Schulmann, Sarah Schulmann, Niklas Svennung (Galerie Chantal Crousel), Elie Wajeman, Sacha Zilberfarb.

All my gratitude to the Paraguay team and the friendship that binds us.

Thanks to the Cnap (Centre National d'Arts Plastiques) for supporting my research in theory and art criticism through a grant obtained in 2017, which enabled me to write this book.

She wasn't there when I started this book but she watched over its conclusion: long live Palma Camporesi Schulmann.

Finally, thanks to Cécile Lee and the whole Les Fugitives team who made it possible for this book to cross the Channel, and without whom the incredible chorus of translators dedicated to bringing it into English, would never have seen the light of day. And so, thank you: Naima Rashid, Natasha Lehrer, Lauren Elkin, Ruth Diver, Jessica Spivey, Jennifer Higgins, Clem Clement and Sophie Lewis.

• Credits •

Citation on p. 73 from Jean-Patrick Manchette, *Fatale* © Editions Gallimard, Paris, 1977, reprinted with permision of the copyright owner.

Extract on p.80 from Anne Sexton's poem 'Consorting with Angels' (1963), in Anne Sexton, *The Complete Poems*, ed. Maxine Kumin, Boston, Houghton Mifflin Company, 1981, p. 111.

Citation on p.117 from Kaja Silverman, *The Acoustic Mirror. The Female Voice in Psychoanalysis and Cinema*, © Indiana University Press, 1988. Reprinted with permission of Indiana University Press.

Citation on pp.128–29 from Lauren Berlant, 'The Female Complaint', in *Social Text*, vol. 7, no. 1–2 (19/20), pp. 237–259, copyright 1988, *Social Text*. Reprinted by permission of the copyright holder, and the Publisher Duke University Press.

Citation on p.158 from bell hooks, 'Choosing the Margin as a Space of Radical Openness' in *Yearnings: Race, Gender and Cultural Politics*, Routledge, 1989. Reprinted with permission of Taylor & Francis.

Citation on p.173 from Anne Carson, *Glass, Irony, and God*, copyright © 1995. Reprinted by permission of New Directions Publishing Corp.

Disclaimer: The publisher warrants that every effort has been made to seek and obtain permission from copyright holders to reprint these and other excerpts cited in this volume at time of publication, for those citations that may not be considered fair use. Any omissions will be rectified immediately upon written notification to Les Fugitives by the copyright holder or their representative

Clara Schulmann has been working as a contemporary art critic for over fifteen years. Her writing tells of meetings, exchanges and collaborations with artists. She has taught art theory in a number of universities, including the Paris Beaux-arts. She also holds a doctorate in film studies, for her thesis *Les Chercheurs d'or* (Gold Diggers). Her first book *Films d'artistes, histoires de l'art* was published in France in 2014 by Les presses du réel. *Chicanes* is her first book to be published in English.

• Translators •

Clem Clement graduated in 2019 from Brasenose College, Oxford, with a degree in French and Persian. She gathered translation experience through her editorial role for Les Fugitives, as well as freelance copy-editing for the Poetry Foundation. *Chicanes* marks her first contribution to a published translation. She lives in Norfolk.

Ruth Diver holds a Doctorate in French and Comparative Literature from the University of Auckland

and University of Paris VII, published as *Enfants russes, écrivains français*. As the former head of the comparative literature programme at the University of Auckland, she has published research on translingual authors. She is the winner of the 2016 Asymptote Close Approximations Fiction Prize for her translation of *Maraude* by Sophie Pujas, and of French Voices Awards for *Titus Did Not Love Berenice* by Nathalie Azoulai and *Marx and the Doll* by Maryam Madjidi. Her recent translations include *A Respectable Occupation*, by Julia Kerninon for Les Fugitives; *In Eve's Attire*, by Delphine Horvilleur; *Beirut 2020: the Collapse of a Civilization, a Journal*, by Charif Majdalani; and *The Little Girl on the Ice Floe*, by Adélaïde Bon. She lives in Aotearoa, New Zealand.

Lauren Elkin is a Franco-American writer and translator, most recently of Simone de Beauvoir's previously unpublished novel *The Inseparables*. Her co-translation (with Charlotte Mandell) of Claude Arnaud's biography of Jean Cocteau won the 2017 French American Foundation's translation prize. She is also the author of *No. 91/92: Notes on a Parisian Commute* and *Flâneuse: Women Walk the City*, which was a finalist for the PEN/Diamonstein-Spielvogel award for the art of the essay, a *New York Times* Notable Book of 2017, and a Radio 4 Book of the Week. Her essays have appeared in *Granta*, the *London Review of Books*, *Harper's*, the *New York*

Clara Schulmann

Times, and *The White Review*, among others. She lives in London.

Jennifer Higgins translates from French and Italian. She has recently produced the first translation of Jean Lorrain's 1906 play, *Ennoïa*. With Sophie Lewis, she has co-translated two books by Emmanuelle Pagano, including *Faces on the Tip of my Tongue*, longlisted for the International Booker Prize 2020. Other translations include *The Photographer of Auschwitz*, and *A Short Philosophy of Birds*. Jennifer was programme manager for the Queen's College Translation Exchange from its inception in 2018 until 2021 and is a collaborator in the ongoing Decadence in Translation research network based at Glasgow University. She has been a mentor for the Peirene Stevns Translation Prize and is a tutor on the Oxford University Advanced French Translation course. She lives in Oxford.

Sophie Lewis translates from French and Portuguese. She has translated Stendhal, Jules Verne, Marcel Aymé, Violette Leduc, Leïla Slimani, Noémi Lefebvre, Mona Chollet, Emmanuelle Pagano and Colette Fellous, as well as Natalia Borges Polesso, João Gilberto Noll, Sheyla Smanioto and Patrícia Melo, among others. She has been long- and shortlisted for the Scott Moncrieff, the Republic of Consciousness and the International Booker prizes, and was joint winner of the 2022 French-American Foundation

203

non-fiction prize for *In the Eye of the Wild* by the anthropologist Nastassja Martin. She co-founded the translation workshops enterprise Shadow Heroes. While senior editor at And Other Stories, she edited Deborah Levy's breakout novel *Swimming Home*, and she was most recently managing editor at the Folio Society. She lives in London.

Naima Rashid is a UK-based Pakistani author and poet, whose writings in English have appeared in *Asymptote*, *The Scores*, *Wild Court, Litro,* and many other places. She was longlisted for the National Poetry Competition 2019 (UK) and Best Small Fictions 2022 (USA). A translator from Urdu, her past and forthcoming publications include the acclaimed *Defiance of the Rose* by Perveen Shakir, and *Naulakhi Kothi* by Ali Akbar Natiq. Naima has worked between French and English for over a decade and has been affiliated with the linguistic departments of the French Cultural Centres in Jeddah and Lahore. She has taught French as a foreign language with the Alliance Française and French literature at university level and is a contributor to the translation educational initiative Shadow Heroes.

Jessie Spivey is an occasional translator from French into English. She has previously worked on projects for Emmaus International, Il Cinema Ritrovato and Les Fugitives & Hotel Magazine collaboration

Detour/Détours. As part of her role with Les Fugitives, where she started as an intern in 2017, she has supported the publication of many translations from the French. She currently works as a literary publicist, and lives in London.

Founded in 2014 Les Fugitives is a London-based independent press for contemporary literary fiction and narrative non-fiction in translation, mostly by francophone women writers critically acclaimed in France, and previously unpublished in English.

In 2021, Les Fugitives published Lauren Elkin's *No. 91/92: notes on a Parisian commute*, which spurred the creation, in 2022, of 'the quick brown fox' collection, dedicated to new writing in English.

Also published by Les Fugitives, in 'the quick brown fox' collection:

Erica van Horn
We Still Have the Telephone

In translation from the French:
Ananda Devi
Eve out of Her Ruins; *The Living Days*
trans. Jeffrey Zuckerman

Maylis de Kerangal
Eastbound
trans. Jessica Moore

Colette Fellous
This Tilting World
trans. Sophie Lewis

Jean Frémon
Now, Now, Louison; *Nativity*
trans. Cole Swensen

Mireille Gansel
Translation as Transhumance
trans. Ros Schwartz

Julia Kerninon
A Respectable Occupation
trans. Ruth Diver

Camille Laurens
Little Dancer Aged Fourteen
trans. Willard Wood

Noémi Lefebvre
Blue Self-Portrait; *Poetics of Work*
trans. Sophie Lewis

Nathalie Léger
Suite for Barbara Loden; *Exposition*; *The White Dress*
trans. Natasha Lehrer & C. Menon; Amanda
DeMarco; N. Lehrer

Lucie Paye
Absence
trans. Natasha Lehrer

Anne Serre
The Governesses; *The Fool and Other Moral Tales*
trans. Mark Hutchinson

Shumona Sinha
Down with the Poor!
trans. Teresa Lavender Fagan

Sylvie Weil
Selfies
trans. Ros Schwartz

• www.lesfugitives.com •